The Detroit Pistons
1991-92

by Roland Lazenby

Photographs by Kirthmon Dozier
of *The Detroit News*

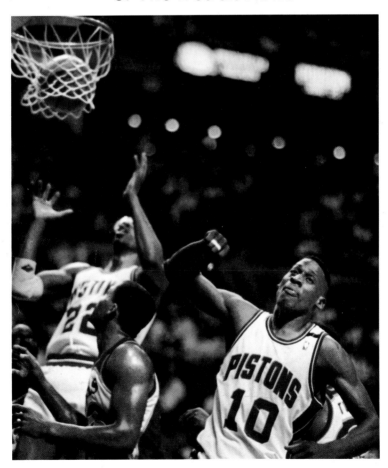

TAYLOR PUBLISHING COMPANY
Dallas, Texas

Design by Karen Snidow Lazenby

©1991, Roland Lazenby
Taylor Publishing Company
1550 West Mockingbird Lane, Dallas, Texas 75235

Library of Congress Cataloging-in-Publication Data

Lazenby, Roland.
        The Detroit Pistons : 1991-92 / Roland Lazenby.
                p.   cm.
        ISBN 0-87833-034-8
        1. Detroit Pistons (Basketball team)   I. Title

Printed in the United States of America

Contents

The big accomplishment of the 1991 season was a playoff win over Boston.

Preface

Welcome to the fourth edition of the Detroit Pistons yearbook. As with previous editions, it reflects the efforts and involvement of many people.

Many thanks go to the Detroit Pistons' public relations staff—Matt Dobek, Sue and Dave Wieme. Matt compiled the information for Piston Profiles and wrote the bios.

In addition, I want to recognize the editorial assistance of Bob Hartman.

Much credit goes to Arnold Hanson, the publisher at Taylor Publishing Company who first suggested this project and who continues to support it.

A number of people were gracious in granting interviews, most of which were brief post-game, locker-room sessions. They include Bill Laimbeer, Joe Dumars, Dennis Rodman, Mark Aguirre, Isiah Thomas, and Chuck Daly.

The book would be drab were it not for the outstanding photographic contributions of Kirthmon Dozier. And the staff at Taylor Publishing has carried the production load with professionalism.

Extensive use was made of a variety of publications, including the *Chicago Tribune, Chicago Sun Times, The Detroit News, The Detroit Free Press, Flint Journal, The Oakland Press, Los Angeles Times, The National, The Oregonian, Sport, Sports Illustrated*, and *The Sporting News.*

The work of a variety of beat writers and columnists has been a vital aid in this project. That group includes the following: Mitch Albom, Bryan Burwell, Shelby Strother, Charlie Vincent, Drew Sharp, Terry Foster, Steve Addy, Dean Howe, Bob Wojnowski, Corky Meinecke, Steve Kornacki, Bill Halls, Joe Falls, Jerry Green, and Michelle Kaufmann.

Roland Lazenby

September 1990

Pain And No Gain

T he Fort Wayne Pistons won back-to-back championships in the old National Basketball League in 1944 and '45. Like the modern Pistons, this older version was a guard-oriented team that liked to intimidate opponents.

During the 1946 playoffs, the Pistons went for a third straight championship and stumbled, losing decisively to the Rochester Royals.

Alas, history repeated itself in 1991.

Like their Fort Wayne ancestors, the Detroit Pistons were going for a third straight professional championship. But their drive came to a rather decisive halt against Michael Jordan and the Chicago Bulls in the Eastern Conference Finals.

A combination of factors brought the demise of the 1991 Pistons, but more than anything else it seemed to be the cumulative wear and tear from their two straight championship seasons. Isiah Thomas underwent wrist surgery in Janaury 1991, and although he returned in time for the playoffs, the team never quite regained its full strength.

The Pistons did, however, pull off quite a feat in the post-season, that being the come-from-behind victory over the Boston Celtics in the Eastern semifinals. Long-time Pistons fans know that for years the Celtics owned Motown. There was a time when the Beantown bunch regularly took the Pistons' lunch money and bullied them.

But that all changed in 1988 when the Bad Boys went into Boston Garden and whipped the Celtics, claiming the Eastern Conference crown in the process. For Detroit purposes, that 1988 Eastern Conference series was known as Garden Party I.

Garden Party II followed in 1989, but it wasn't nearly as much fun. Larry Bird was out with injuries, and the Pistons quickly felled the Celtics, 3-0, in the first round of the Eastern playoffs.

The 1991 playoffs brought Garden Party III, a battle of two proud but injured teams. Both Zeke and Larry Legend missed some action. The Pistons fell behind 2-1 in games, and Boston had the homecourt advantage. In years past, that would have sent Celtics President Red

The Pistons have found a comfort zone in Boston Garden. (Lipofsky photo).

Aguirre takes a seat.

Whatever happened in the NBA in 1991, teams around the league wanted to make sure the Pistons didn't win three straight.

Auerbach reaching for another cigar.

But for years, Isiah had been lecturing anyone who would listen that Detroit needed to build Pistons' Pride to match Auerbach's tradition and Celtics' Pride. Well, Isiah finally made his point in the Eastern semifinals. The Pistons were weary and hurting and could have easily packed it in. Instead, they summoned what they had and fought to three straight wins to claim the series, 4-2.

Like magic, Detroit had done it again. Garden Party III.

The Pistons had gotten their lunch money back.

With interest.

PRESSURE

Whatever happened in the NBA in 1991, teams around the league wanted to make sure the Pistons didn't win three straight championships. Everywhere the Bad Boys went, they found intense competition. Isiah had never seen, or felt, anything like it. "Teams and individuals have never played harder against me since I've been in the league," he said.

A case in point was Detroit's early December game against the Lakers in Los Angeles. "We came back out at halftime," Thomas said, "and James Worthy was screaming at Magic, 'All right! 24 minutes! 24 minutes and we got 'em!' That's just an indication of how intense people were against us, because you usually only hear talk like that during the playoffs."

The Pistons opened December with four straight road losses and quickly realized that they were

heading into new territory. "Since I've been here," forward Mark Aquirre said, "we've never lost four straight games before."

How quickly things had changed. In 1990, the Pistons won the title by using their quick guards to "break opponents down off the dribble." But just six months later, they were stumbling through a dismal December, and their coaches felt that the guards were resorting to too much one-on-one basketball. In a practice, Chuck Daly declared it was time for the guards to dispense with the one-on-one play and start passing the ball and working the offense again.

The Pistons were losing for a variety of reasons, said assistant coach Brendan Malone. "But if you want to look for a common denominator through this streak, it's that we're not shooting the ball well, particularly our guards."

Both Isiah Thomas and Vinnie Johnson had hit only 42 percent of

Mark led the charge against Boston, averaging 19.7 points.

The Worm stalks Larry.

their shots. "Joe Dumars is shooting about 47 percent," Malone said, "but he's been up and down."

Yet the problem didn't rest solely with the guards. They'd been forced to play more one-on-one basketball because the team's half-court offense and the post play hadn't been consistent. Whenever center James Edwards got off to a good start in a game, the Pistons usually went on to win. But Edwards was plagued by injuries and foul trouble, which left Daly searching among his players for an effective chemistry.

The team, though, was used to experimenting. As Bill Laimbeer pointed out, the Pistons had evolved through the past two regular seasons

They ran up a 6-9 record in December, but true to their forecasts, the Pistons opened the new year with 11 straight wins. Which was good enough to take them to the Central Division lead.

toward championship form. "The last two years, we've had different lineups and won championships," he said after a December loss in Boston Garden. "This year we have the same lineup as last year, but it doesn't seem to be effective right now. We have to find out who can play and in what situations he can play in. So we're searching for combinations that will work. And we're real good at that. We'll find it. It might take us a while. We may lose a few games. But when we find our groove, find our niche, we'll be right there."

A big part of their troubles stemmed from their schedule, which included two early West Coast trips.

The Pistons knew their schedule grew softer after Christmas. They planned to catch up then. After all, the past two springs had brought impressive winning streaks on the way to rings and excitement.

"It's a long season," Isiah Thomas said. "I'd rather start out shooting 40

Spider hooks.

percent and end up high than start out high and tail off toward the end of the season when things are important."

They ran up a 6-9 record in December, but true to their forecasts, the Pistons opened the new year with 11 straight wins. Which was good enough to take them to the Central Division lead. They paused there at the crest of the hump and seemed on course for another 60-win season.

However, their fortunes plummeted

with startling swiftness. Isiah had seen it coming in early December. After a loss at Utah, Thomas awakened Daly with a 4 a.m. phone call. He felt he was carrying too much leadership responsibility for the team. What he didn't tell Daly was that his right wrist was killing him. He had aggravated an old injury, and the soreness and swelling increased. Then, two games later, in Sacramento, he fell on the wrist, making it worse.

The Pistons didn't go down gently.

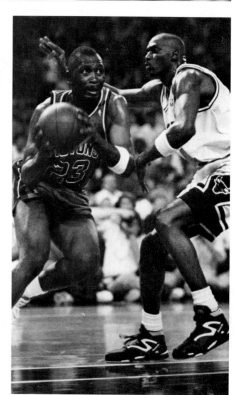

To the hole.

Making Patrick pay.

INJURED RESERVE

The wrist was actually just one of Isiah's ailments. During the preseason, he ruptured the tear duct valve in his eye and underwent surgery. For the next 12 weeks, he played with a plastic tube in his tear duct that altered his vision. He attempted to wear goggles to protect the injury, but found them distracting.

Then in mid January, he suffered a painful groin injury during a close game in Houston. Throughout the five weeks since his wrist injury, the swelling and pain had grown, leaving his fingers stiff and virtually immovable. Still he attempted to

Daly knew tough times were ahead. For the first time in five seasons, they lost five straight games. They also lost three straight home games, something fans at the Palace had never seen.

play in a January 23rd game at Boston. He couldn't perform, and afterward Joe Dumars told him it was time for wrist surgery.

Isiah knew he was right.

The bones in his wrist were fused in surgery January 29, a delicate procedure that could have ended his career. At the very least, the surgery had probably ended Isiah's season, doctors predicted. For the first time in his career, Thomas was placed on injured reserve.

Daly knew tough times were ahead. For the first time in five seasons, they lost five straight games. They also lost three straight home games, something fans at the Palace had never seen.

With Isiah's wrist came a host of other injuries. Dumars, who carried the load in Isiah's absence, was hobbled by a hyperextended toe. John Salley was out seven games with a back injury, while Edwards was also troubled by his back and

Dennis matches up with all sizes.

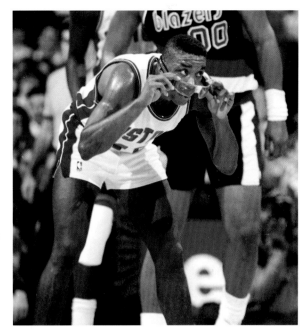
Isiah didn't like the goggles.

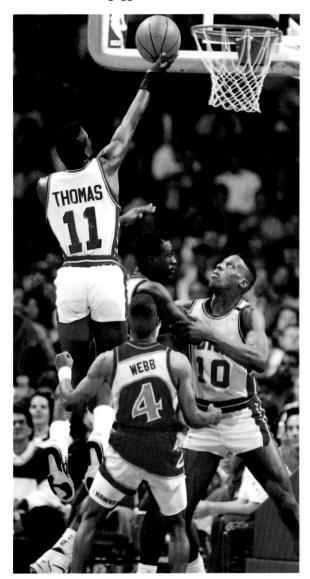
Thomas led the comeback against Atlanta.

Bedford looks to score.

Laimbeer was slowed with a sore knee.

To fill the gap, General Manager Jack McCloskey signed the old stand-bys, John Long and Gerald Henderson.

"It was my job to keep the whole thing together," Daly told Corky Meinecke of the *Free Press*. "And some days I'm not as good at that as others... I told the players that the key word for the season was going to be tolerance. But no matter how much you talk about it, it gets difficult. And Isiah's injury made it worse."

There were other complications. Both Edwards and Aguirre wanted raises. And Laimbeer became concerned that he no longer played a major offensive role.

Isiah returned to action by April 5, but by then the Pistons were already 8 1/2 games behind the Bulls. He immediately assumed the role of the feiry leader. Within days of his return, he was blasting his teammates and the coaches.

"Nobody gives a [bleep] anymore," he told a group of writers. "There are too many different agendas."

His criticism also implied that Daly was being distracted by his selection as the 1992 U.S. Olympic coach. The outburst brought a long talk with Daly at practice at Oakland University April 12. "I still feel the same as I did yesterday," Thomas said afterward. "We've just got to get better as a team. The only thing that is going to help me is winning. Until we start winning, I'm going to stay mad."

"We're all subject to the circle of blame," Daly admitted. "I think he was frustrated when he said those things. We had a talk to discuss a few matters, but it's nothing that a few wins won't cure."

As for his Olympic involvement, Daly was privately angry at the implication he wasn't doing his job. In fact, he and his assistants felt that they had done perhaps their best coaching job ever in the wake of the team's injuries and dissension. "I don't think that had anything to do with it," Daly said of his Olympic activities. "All I've done is attend one meeting and look at some films."

Thomas, however, refused to back down. "We can't just keep fooling ourselves that things are just magically going to turn around by playoff time," he said. "Someday we've got to get started to getting back to business."

In retrospect, they were both right. They badly needed to regroup as a team, as Thomas said. But that wouldn't be possible, physically and mentally.

They struggled to a 52-30 finish, then fought to get past the Atlanta Hawks in the first round of the playoffs. The second round against Boston brought more trouble. But again the Pistons dug their way out of it, eliminating Boston with a 117-113 overtime win in Game 6 of the conference semifinal.

Afterward, Isiah fought through the crowd to catch Celtic forward Kevin McHale. The series was hard-fought but without the rancor that sometimes accompanied Detroit-Boston battles of the past. "I wanted to let him know what a pleasure it was to compete against players like him," Isiah said of McHale. "I couldn't get to Larry, but I told Kevin to tell him the same thing. They make me feel proud to be an athlete."

Isiah had injured his right foot in the playoffs against Boston. At first, doctors thought the injury was a bruise. Two weeks after the season, further examination revealed that Thomas had broken it, and his foot was placed in a cast.

The conference finals with Chicago held no warmth. The Bulls smelled

They couldn't solve the Chicago riddle.

blood and took the first three games with a hauteur. Then on the eve of Game 4 in Detroit, Michael Jordan had this to say about the Pistons:

"The people I know are going to be happy they're not the reigning champions anymore. We'll get back to the image of a clean game. People want to push this kind of basketball [Pistons] out.

"When Boston was the champion, they played true basketball. Detroit

won. You can't take that away from them. But it wasn't clean basketball. It wasn't the kind of basketball you want to endorse. We're not trying to lower ourselves to their kind of play. I may talk some trash, but we're playing hard, clean basketball. They've tried to provoke us, and we've kept our poise."

Jordan concluded his talk by saying, "I think we can sweep this team."

Told of the comment, Isiah fired back, "No, we're not going to get swept."

It happened, of course. The thing that Thomas had feared in April upon his return, the thing he always feared most, had happened.

They had been swept.

By the Bulls.

They returned what they felt was Jordan's insult by walking off the floor at the end, without offering congratulations. Daly had asked them not to do it. The snub angered television viewers and Chicago fans, and it may have even cost Isiah a chance to compete on the Olympic team.

But they weren't about to shake

> **It happened, of course. The thing that Thomas had feared in April upon his return, the thing he always feared most, had happened.**
> **They had been swept.**
> **By the Bulls.**

Michael's hand. He had insulted their accomplishments. Even Joe Dumars, who had a good relationship with Jordan, was angry.

The anger burned with the hurt, and the mixture was the worst possible for the Bad Boys.

Their only hope was that the worst would spur them to the best for 1992. Some would say it was a long, dim hope. They were aging, and General Manager Jack McCloskey was poised to change the roster.

So much was unknown. Who would go. Who would stay. Perhaps the greatest unknown lay in Isiah's character. How deep was his character? Could he will them a third championship?

This much was sure. It would take another championship to ease this pain.

The Chicago loss hurt.

Will Chuck and Zeke figure out how to win another title?

The Big Squeeze

It's a bit of a stretch to feel sorry for Chuck Daly. After all, he makes about a million bucks a year. And he's the grand dandy of them all, wearing the finest threads in a business of silk hankies and $700 suits. Best of all, he gets to coach the greatest team ever.

Not the Pistons.

The NBA Olympic Gold. (If Miami can be the Heat, our Olympic team can be the Gold.) Unless you've just returned from an isolation cell, you probably know that for the first time America will be able to include NBA' players on its Olympic team.

There's Michael and Magic and Larry and Karl and Charles and Scottie and Chris and John and David and Patrick.

It's the John on this list that could prove to be an enormous complicating factor in Daly's life over the next 10 months. That would be John Stockton, point guard of the Utah Jazz, who has led the league in assists for the past four seasons.

Isiah Thomas, of course, has led the league in championships during that same time frame. Well, not entirely by himself. But, if anything, last season proved that Thomas was the central ingredient in Detroit's rather curious chemistry.

He certainly deserved a spot on the team but was snubbed by the USA Basketball selection committee.

At best, it creates a terribly uncomfortable situation for Daly. He coaches the Pistons, yet his star player wasn't picked for the team. Daly, of course, has been careful to point out that he wasn't allowed to pick the team. And Detroit General Manager Jack McCloskey, who was on the committee, promptly resigned in protest over the Isiah snub.

But the pressure knob got twisted

The question is not whether the U.S. will be able to win the Olympic gold, but whether the perceived conflicts will wreck the Pistons chances for a third NBA title.

to high in late September when *Sports Illustrated* writer Jack McCallum quoted unnamed sources on the selection committee as saying:

1) Daly had presented a wish list of seven players to the committee, and Isiah wasn't on it.

2) McCloskey had never really pushed for Isiah on the committee and his resignation was a "smokescreen."

3) As part of his informal negotiations for joining the team, Michael Jordan made a stipulation that his old foe, Isiah, not be included.

4) The rationale for not including Thomas is that his personality might be detrimental to the team.

Of these items, number four is pure poppycock. However, the rest of the information could be devastating. As such, it is certainly open to

question. The Pistons have never generated much love among their fellow competitors. If you don't like 'em, what better way to submarine their season than as an unnamed source in *SI*?

Regardless of whether you accept the information provided by McCallum's unnamed sources, you have to acknowledge its impact. The narrow path that Chuck Daly was taking just got narrower. The question is not whether the U.S. will be able to win the Olympic gold, but whether the perceived conflicts will wreck the Pistons' chances for a third NBA title.

First of all, the team is in a state of transition. Long-time regular Vinnie Johnson was released in the offseason and center/forward James Edwards was traded to the Los Angeles Clippers. Forwards Orlando Woolridge (from Denver in a trade for Scott Hastings) and Brad Sellers (a free agent) were brought in to give the team more open-court offense. Darrell Walker was acquired from Washington to bolster the backcourt.

All of which should translate into a different modus operandi for Detroit. The Pistons, a team that badly needs scoring, gave up two of its best scorers, to change gears. The goal is to get away from their plodding approach.

'We realize that to beat Chicago, we have to do more damage in the open floor," Daly said of the changes. He added, however, that it remained to be seen how the new players would fit in.

"Offensively, we'll be able to score more," Thomas offered. "We won't be able to score them in the half-court situation, but I think the defense and our quickness will get us more baskets in transition."

Such changes are difficult enough

to effect in the best of situations. What is the team mindset with the Olympic issue hanging over its head? If last season was any indication, the answer is "troubled."

"We had some moments during the season, some flare-ups," Daly told Corky Meinecke of the *Free Press* in June. "That's going to happen under the best of circumstances. But we never really exploded, and that's a credit to the team and the coaching staff. We were able to handle it and get through it.

"We had a party the Wednesday night following our last game, and Billy [Laimbeer] made a very precise statement to me. He told me he had

"I've never felt such a mix of emotions that I feel right now," Thomas told McCallum in late September when asked about the Olympic selection.

gone to Isiah earlier in the year and said, 'This team is wound too tight.' We were so squeezed. There was pressure from every direction. But we didn't explode.

"Now I think there will be a different air, a different atmosphere. No question about it. But to really get an accurate evaluation of that, we'll have to wait and see what the roster looks like when training camp opens next October."

And that, of course, sums up the Pistons hopes for the 1991-92 season. They've earned a reputation as a mentally tough team. Will they be tough enough to minimize the turmoil? The best answer begins with their team leader.

"I've never felt such a mix of emotions that I feel right now," Thomas told McCallum in late September when asked about the Olympic selection. "It's not the most disappointing moment in my life, but it's close. It's a bitter pill to swallow, and I just want to get the taste out of my mouth as soon as I can.

Finding a new chemistry will occupy the Detroit bench.

Walker came to the backcourt from Washington.

"Daly is not just somebody who has experience at every level, or has the reputation of being able to get along with players," said NBA deputy commissioner Russ Granik. **"The absolute achievement is there."**

"All my career I've done nothing but win. I've always adapted to change, I thought, almost as well as anyone, and I would've adapted for this team. I'd still be honored to chosen, but if I'm not, I'll still be rooting for us to win the gold medal."

Looking for the positive, Piston fans may read a bit between those lines. Translation: The snub has made Isiah more determined than ever. The Pistons have a brutal November and December, one that either crushes them or molds them as championship contenders.

Stay tuned for the results. You couldn't ask for a more dramatic situation.

THE ABSOLUTE ACHIEVEMENT

The controversy over Isiah's selection has clouded a tremendous honor for Daly. His selection as the 1992 U.S. Olympic coach recognizes that he is respected among his peers and viewed as one of the all-time best.

Michael didn't want Isiah on the team.

"It is a job of incredible prestige," Daly conceded. "It may be a once-in-a-lifetime opportunity. If you are a lifer, a guy who has spent his life in coaching, it is the ultimate. Any time you have a chance to do something for your country, it's an honor. This is something you don't dream will ever happen to you. It's beyond dreams."

How can you dream that far ahead when you're the high school coach in Punxsutawney, Pa.? Or an assistant at Duke? Or the head coach at Penn and Boston University? How can you dream about the Olympics when you're the fired coach of the Cleveland Cavaliers?

But it was those experiences that has made Daly what he is today. Once he had coached two world champions in Detroit, the dreaming got a little easier.

It was Daly's accomplishments that got him the job, said C.M. Newton, chairman of the selection committee. "He has been a tremendous coach at all levels."

"He is not just somebody who has experience at every level, or has the reputation of being able to get along with players," said NBA deputy commissioner Russ Granik. "The absolute achievement is there."

Without a doubt, Daly has the portfolio. But more important, he has the temperament to pull all of this talent together. There seems to be little doubt that, with or without Isiah, the 61-year-old Daly will coach the U.S. to the Olympic Gold.

Beyond that, what happens is anyone's guess.

"You know me," he told reporters when asked about the future. "I don't go beyond the next game. You can't be sure what may happen then. Who knows? I may ride off into the sunset after Barcelona."

The Pistons were wrapped a little too tight in 1991.

Vinnie the scrapper.

In traffic.

Eye ball.

The release.

Loose ball.

Hail Vinnie!

And now there are two.

The Detroit Pistons' rise to success began as a threesome during the 1981-82 season. Isiah Thomas arrived in the 1981 draft. Bill Laimbeer showed up in a February deal.

And Vinnie Johnson came from Seattle in a November 21, 1981 trade for Gregory Kelser.

The three of them have seen it all together. When they got here, the Pistons were a lower-rung team. But together, they climbed the NBA ladder, moving right over

Vinnie was a power against Portland in 1990.

The muscle man.

Vinnie, the underrated defender.

the backs of the Celtics and Lakers to snatch two championships. In retrospect, this trio sported a certain symmetry: Isiah as the flash-and-dash wunderkind at the point; Laimbeer the starting center and designated rebounder. And Vinnie as the heat off the bench.

Boy, was he some heat.

Just when the oppositions' tongues were wagging and they were looking for a break, Vinnie stepped up and pushed 'em.

The Celtics always dreaded the moment when Chuck Daly gave Vinnie the nod and he popped out of his warmup. Most NBA players have a healthy respect for Boston Garden.

Not Vinnie.

Chuck Daly will be the first to admit that he never really understood how Vinnie worked. Nobody did. This 6'2" ball of offensive muscle simply defied logic. When Vinnie got into his groove, nobody could stop him.

He trashed the place quicker than anybody in the history of the game.

"The Microwave," Boston's Danny Ainge dubbed him a few years back. "He really heated up in a hurry."

Chuck Daly will be the first to admit that he never really understood how Vinnie worked. Nobody did. This 6'2" ball of offensive muscle simply defied logic. When Vinnie got into his groove, nobody could stop him. Nobody.

Daly was plenty smart to see that, understand him or not, a good team could "ride" Vinnie. Simply put him on the floor and watch him motor the Pistons along.

Quite often, the rest of the team would sit back and enjoy the scenery. "Vinnie is fun when he gets going," Isiah said a few seasons back. "We just tell him to take every shot. We all screen for him and he just goes crazy."

Vinnie never had to be told twice to shoot. Heck, he never had to be told once.

007.

The silent leader.

Determined.

The driver's seat.

The third guard.

Going long.

Riding the Bulls.

"If I hit two or three in a row, I'm going to look for that shot," he once explained. "And I don't care how big or strong he is, I'm gonna take my shot. I am used to taking off-balance shots, shots that would look difficult to other guys. But if I'm shooting it, I'm shooting it."

This bravado was cast during his years on the playgrounds of Brooklyn, where you couldn't call fouls. You had to make your shots no matter how hard you got bumped. Vinnie learned to arch way back, ball hidden behind his head for a deceptive release. How many times have Pistons fans seen a long-armed opponent reach back there for the ball while Vinnie still gets the shot off anyway? How many times have they seen it swish.

At the close of last season, Vinnie had rung up 10,173 regular-season points for the Pistons, just about all of them while coming off Detroit's bench. Few people doubt that he could have scored far more as a starter on another team.

There are many injustices in life, and the NBA has its share. How unfair is it that the Microwave played a decade as a sixth man yet never won the league's Sixth Man Award?

He helped sweep the Lakers in '89.

The closest he came was the 1986-87 season when he finished second in the balloting behind Ricky Pierce of Milwaukee.

After Detroit won its second title in 1991, Laimbeer went to Vinnie and thanked him personally for his sacrifice. "Vinnie Johnson could have been an All-Star if he played on a team where he is the go-to man," Laimbeer said. "He has sacrificed his entire game throughout his whole career for the Detroit Piston

At the close of last season, Vinnie had rung up 10,173 regular-season points for the Pistons, just about all of them while coming off Detroit's bench.

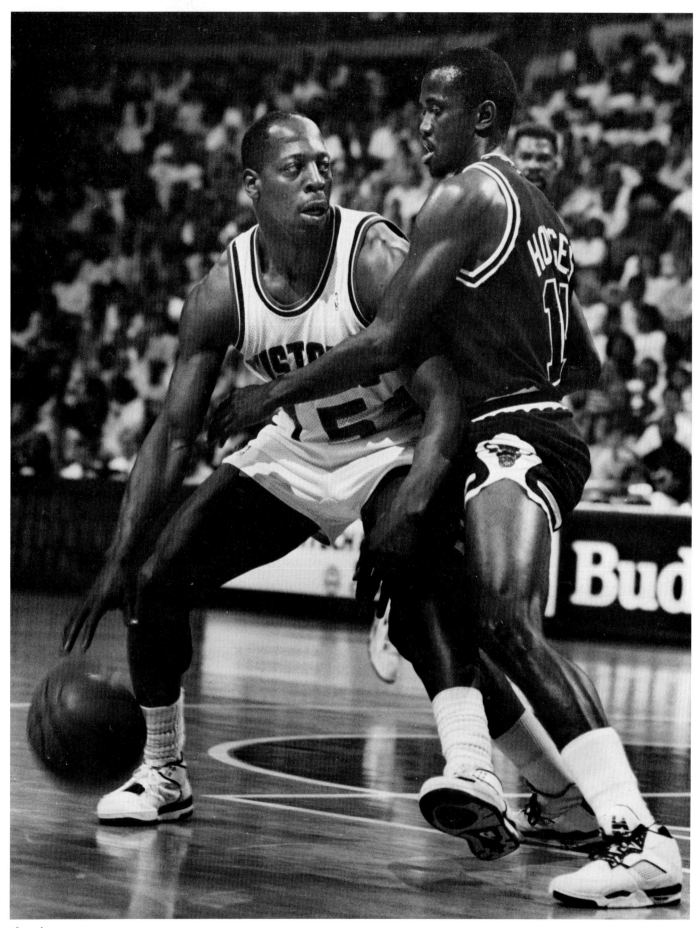

A pro's pro.

organization, and he's one of my favorite individuals."

Vinnie was asked about his sacrifice in 1989. "Sometimes I think about not getting some of the credit or respect I deserve," he replied. "But that's just part of the business."

The "business" finally caught up with Vinnie over the offseason. Pistons management decided he was too old and too expensive to keep on the roster. That's an end that all athletes face, no matter how talented

and popular and self-sacrificing they may be.

But it doesn't dim the 10 years of contributions Vinnie made to the team. In acknowledgment of that, PISTONS YEARBOOK would like to say, "Hail to the 'Wave.'"

Thanks, Vinnie, for all those jumpers. Thanks for the 19 straight points against Utah in '89. Thanks for the shot with 0.07 seconds on the clock to win the 1990 title.

But thanks most of all for your

understated greatness, night in, night out.

They won't miss you in Boston. And that's the greatest compliment.

"The players around the league fear him," Isiah said a few years back. "It seems like every time we play the Celtics, Vinnie gets on fire. He gives them that double pump. DJ will have his hand on the ball, and Vinnie will take it out of his hand and bury it. From like 20 feet."

Reach. (Lipofsky photo).

Moving the ball.

The Bill Is Due

February 16, 1992 will mark the 10th anniversary of Bill Laimbeer's appearance in a Pistons uniform. His entrance wasn't exactly trumpeted back in February 1982. In the midst of his second NBA season, he came from Cleveland in a trade that left people scratching their heads. The teams hastily worked out the deal just nine minutes before the trading deadline.

The Cadavers gave Detroit Laimbeer and Kenny Carr, and the Pistons forked over Phil Hubbard, Paul Mokeski, and first and second round draft choices for 1982. That seemed like a heavy price.

The Iron man.

Vintage Bill.

At the time, Carr appeared to be the front end of the deal. A former first round draft choice of the Lakers (the sixth player taken in 1977), Carr finished out the season with Detroit and moved on to Portland.

Laimbeer, of course, remained.

In many fans' minds, he was just another unknown stiff. But to management, the 6'11" Laimbeer seemed like a solid prospect. Good defensive rebounder. Not much of an "athlete." He had gotten 2,463 minutes of playing time as a rookie with the Cavaliers and had 9.8 points and 8.6 rebounds to show for it.

At the time, Pistons management suffered no delusions that they had

Last season, Laimbeer became the team's all-time leading rebounder, passing Bob Lanier's mark of 8,063. Lanier, as you probably know, had pretty big shoes to fill. But it seems Laimbeer is still filling them.

struck gold in Laimbeer. But time has shown that they did find a pretty impressive vein of iron.

Both in his will and his body.

He has played in 766 games for Detroit and started 765 of them at center. Heading into the 1991-92 season, Laimbeer has missed just three games over his 897-game NBA career.

He missed one game his rookie year at Cleveland due to a coach's decision.

Dumb decision.

He missed two more games as a Piston due to suspension for fighting.

Dumb fight.

Otherwise, Laimbeer might have completed his entire NBA career without having failed to step up for the opening bell (he owns the league's fourth longest consecutive-games-played streak at 685).

Regardless, he has been incredibly consistent and dependable, two highly prized traits in a business

Laimbeer loves competition.

Boxing out Bird. (Lipofsky photo)

Another board. (Lipofsky photo).

where sometimes diapers seem better suited than jock straps.

Last season, he became the team's all-time leading rebounder, passing Bob Lanier's mark of 8,063. Lanier, as you probably know, had pretty big shoes to fill. But it seems Laimbeer is still filling them. Heading into 1991-92, he has 8,504 Piston rebounds. His career total stands at 9,474, and barring an injury or a sudden, unforseen urge to go play golf, Laimbeer will wipe the glass for

board number 10,000 sometime during the campaign.

Not bad.

Some observers have quibbled that after seven straight years of leading the Pistons in rebounding, Laimbeer has relinquished that distinction the past two seasons to board-hungry Dennis Rodman.

That's a sniveling detail.

The big stiff has long ago paid off for Detroit. In retrospect, the Pistons probably should have antied up

another first round pick or so to make the Cavs feel better about the deal.

In fact, many Piston fans would probably agree that the Bill is due.

No, make that "overdue."

So the next time he hits one of those tippy-toes treys of his, or takes a charge, or pulls down a defensive board with his inverted grimace, give Laimbeer a little extra applause, a little more noise.

After a decade, he's earned it.

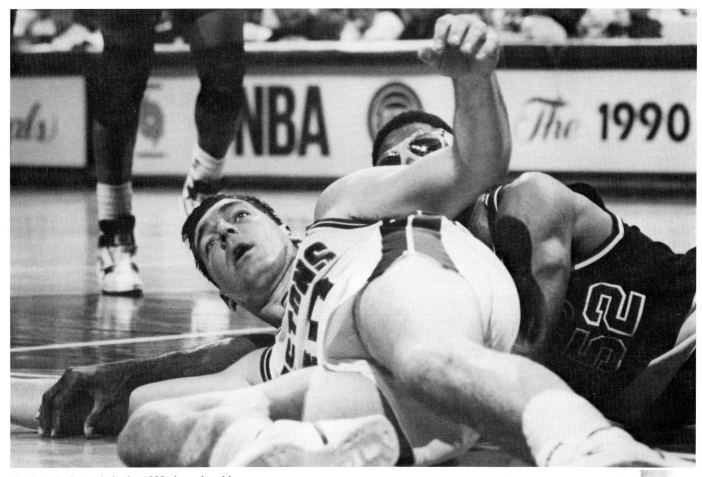

He played a key role in the 1990 championship.

He's a crafty center.

And a decent shooter.

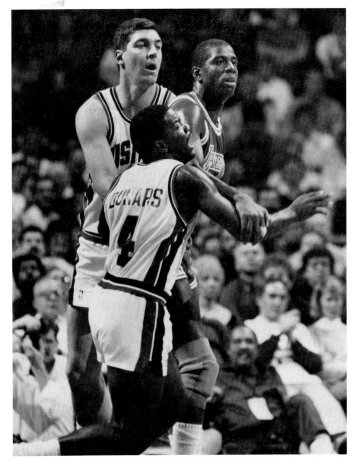

A decade in Detroit.

Dumars led the Pistons in Isiah's absence.

A Talk With Joe

Each of his six NBA seasons, Joe Dumars has increased his scoring average while continuing to boost his excellent all-around play. For 1990-91, he averaged a team-high 20.4 points, each and every one of them badly needed by the Pistons.

When Isiah Thomas went on the injured list after wrist surgery in January, the full load fell on Dumars. As a result, he played 3,046 minutes over 80 regular-season games, the first time since the 1985-86 season (when Isiah Thomas did it) that a Piston had played that much.

Dumars has seldom, if ever, complained during his career. The same was true last season despite the workload. Yet as the season closed, his name was among several Pistons mentioned in trade rumors. In the following off-season interview, he discussed those developments and others.

He was asked about the U.S. Olympic team for 1992, to be coached by Chuck Daly. Dumars said he would like very much to be selected, but if that didn't happen "you'll never hear a word out of me about it."

In an age of high-priced, sometimes spoiled athletes, Dumars has established a reputation for being down to earth. He attributes that to his mother, Ophelia, and his late father, Joe Dumars II.

Q. You played better than 3,000 minutes last season. Athletes are known to want their playing time. But what's it like to play 3,000 minutes? Was it too much?

A. There's nothing more grueling than playing against the best athletes in the world night after night after

After Isiah went down with his injury, I knew I was gonna have to play long minutes. There was nothing to do but get prepared for it.

night and being out there for 40, 45 sometimes 48 of the 48 minutes. It becomes a mind game just to get through it. Your body can't do it alone. It requires mental stamina as well.

Q. What helped you get by?

A. I didn't stay in the locker room before games. I'd always go into a little room by myself. My preparation was different for different games. In some games, the crowd would be pumped up, the team would be pumped up, but I couldn't get too pumped up or I'd lose sight of my game. Those games where everything is hyped and going 100 miles per hour, those were the games where I'd go back, put on my headphones and listen to jazzy, mellow music. I'd go in the back and

listen to some Luther VanDross so I could calm down and make sure I was in control.

If the game was tough to get up for, a game against a lower echelon team, then I'd put on something upbeat, just to get something generated.

Q. Would you want to play 3,000 minutes again this season?

A. Only out of dire necessity. I'm glad I played 3,000 minutes. I'm glad I got to find out what it was like. I don't think it was just the 3,000 minutes that left me so fatigued, though. I think it was what I had to do on the court for those 3,000 minutes. There are guys who played 3,000 minutes who did not have to play the point and play the two guard and guard the other team's best player all at the same time, to generate everything on the floor. It wasn't just the 3,000 minutes; it was everything I had to do.

After Isiah went down with his injury, I knew I was gonna have to play long minutes. There was nothing to do but get prepared for it.

Q. Describe last season in a nutshell.

A. Mental fatigue and injury just seemed to rip through our team. That's a bad combination.

Q. After the Pistons came back against Boston, did you guys think you could go on to win it all again?

A. In everybody's mind, we felt so certain that we could beat Boston, go back and beat Chicago and win it again. There was no doubt in anyone's mind. But I learned this year more than any other year that your body is a precious commodity. Sometimes no matter what your mind is telling you, your body has to be ready. Last year our bodies weren't ready to do what our minds were telling us. The fatigue set in. We just had to walk.

Q. You've come to enjoy a friendly relationship with Michael Jordan. Did the end of last season hurt or embarrass you?

A. No, it didn't hurt or embarrass me. It surprised me. I was disappointed during the Eastern Conference championship series that he started bad-mouthing what our championships had meant to us. If you haven't ever won a championship, or been in another person's shoes, you can't judge what

Sometimes no matter what your mind is telliing you, your body has to be ready. Last year our bodies weren't ready to do what our minds were telling us. The fatigue set in. We just had to walk.

something means to them.

I was disappointed that he had taken it upon himself to explain to the world what Detroit's championships had meant. I Ie's never played here; he's never lived here. So he couldn't possibly know what the championships meant to the city and to the team.

Q. Were you surprised at how good the Bulls were?

A. I knew they were getting better. Much better. I didn't know if they were ready to play the type of ball they played. But they proved that they were. They played exceptionally well.

Q. Sometimes it seemed that the Pistons were so intent on stopping Jordan that they forgot to defend his teammates. Did you guys concentrate too much on Jordan?

A. I haven't looked at the tapes of the series much, but that could be possible. You have to put the majority

Dumars is part of the Pistons' strong leadership.

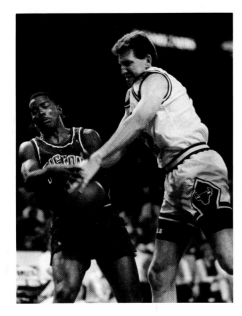

of your focus on him. It's hard to go onto the floor and not focus on that guy, because he can dominate so much of what happens.

It's hard to walk on the floor and not think about what he's going to do.

Q. Is he the greatest player in the NBA today?

A. I think so. I can't think of anybody I've played against who's better.

Q. Much has been made of Isiah's dislike for Jordan. Do you sense it?

A. Isiah has never said to me, "I hate Michael Jordan." He has said to me, "I hate losing." Regardless of who it was, Isiah would have hated losing that series. That's what I make of the situation.

Q. In the wake of last season, did the Pistons need to be overhauled?

A. That's a tough call, because the last five years we've been either the top team in the league or among the top two or three teams. Last year we went to the conference finals. That meant there were only four teams left.

That in itself made a case for allowing things to remain status quo. But I could see moves being made because you have to have turnover, and you have to have fresh people.

Q. What will it take to open up the offense?

A. If we're healthy, we can do

Dumars averaged a career high 20.4 points per game last year.

If anyone can defend Jordan, Joe can.

Joe was surprised by Jordan's talk during last year's Eastern Conference Finals.

more things, we can open up some individually. We can create more. When you're injured, you're limited in what you can do physically. Things tend to get stagnant.

If we're healthy, our offense will open up.

Q. Several names were associated with trade rumors, including yours. Do you think [General Manager] Jack McCloskey is trying to motivate people?

A. I can't think of any reason he would feel he needed to motivate me. I think I have steadily improved every year. They get 100 percent out of me when I step on the floor. I don't see the reason for motivation.

If we're healthy, we can do more things, we can open up some individually. We can create more. When you're injured, you're limited in what you can do physically.

Q. Was it tough to hear your named mentioned in trade rumors?

A. It isn't an easy situation. But I've never been disillusioned about my role here. I understand who I am for this team. If you understand your role for this team, it doesn't surprise you. It disappoints you somewhat.

Q. What exactly is your role in Detroit?

A. I came here in strictly a supporting role, to do whatever needed to be done, and worked my way into a major role, one of the focal points. But that doesn't necessarily mean you are untouchable, or that you have a spot engraved on this team. I realize that.

I'm not one of the people making the decisions. It's disappointing when you give so much. You hear a lot about selfish athletes, and I've never been a selfish athlete. But when you hear talk like this, it makes you start to empathize with the so-called "selfish athlete."

Dumars can play either guard position.

Q. Do you see the loss to Chicago as a motivating factor for this team?

A. This has always been a motivated team. I see no need for rejuvenating around here. We got back to the Eastern Conference finals last year. We ran out of gas. We were tired and hurt and beat up, not just from last season. It was a cumulative thing from the past four or five seasons.

The loss was a knock, but I don't think we have to go around reassessing ourselves. I think if a healthy Pistons team comes back this year, we'll be right back in contention.

The Isiah Decade

T he close of the 1991 campaign marked the tenth season that Isiah Lord Thomas II has spent in the National Basketball Association.

In that time he has put up some impressive numbers. Like 17,321 points.

And 8,381 assists (third in NBA history behind Magic Johnson and Oscar Robertson).

With 3,338 rebounds.

Plus 1,781 steals.

And even 248 blocked shots.

Those numbers would have been even fatter had he not missed 34 games last season due to injuries and subsequent wrist surgery. More specifically, he would likely have become the Pistons all-time leading regular-season scorer. (Currently he ranks 359 points behind Bob Lanier's 15,488 points, and barring injury will pass Lanier during the 1991-92 season.)

But that's okay. Isiah's career hasn't been about numbers anyway. He decided a few years back to trash

Thomas with Boston assistant Don Casey. Lipofsky photo.

Isiah proved the little man had a big place in the game.

his pretty statistics and go after what really mattered.

Winning.

The Pistons have won 564 games since Isiah arrived in Detroit's training camp in 1981.

Three of those wins have earned the Bad Boys Eastern Conference titles.

And two more have brought them back-to-back NBA World Championships.

For Pistons fans, the memories are just as special as the wins:

• The 1984 playoffs against New York, when he scored 16 points in 94 seconds in a furious fourth-quarter rally.

• The 25 points he scored in the

If anything, Isiah Thomas has been defined by his spirit, which is to say that he isn't defined much at all, because from all appearances, his spirit seems boundless.

third quarter (an NBA Finals record) of Game 6 against the Lakers in the 1988 championship series, many of those coming on a severely sprained ankle.

• The 24 points he scored in a quarter during the 1987 playoffs against the Hawks.

• His 16-point barrage against the Trail Blazers in Game 1 of the 1990 Finals, rallying the Pistons from 10 points down.

If anything, Isiah Thomas has been defined by his spirit, which is to say that he isn't defined much at all, because from all appearances, his spirit seems boundless. The pro basketball media have been probing it for a decade now, and they still haven't discovered any sort of dimensions.

They just know it's there.

It used to be that spirit in pro basketball was the exclusive property of the Boston Celtics and Los Angeles Lakers, of Larry Bird and Magic Johnson. They were thought to

For years, Isiah stalked Bird and the Celtics. (Lipofsky photo).

have special magical properties, which no one else could possess.

But then Isiah and the Pistons forced their way into the picture. And the basketball public had to take them seriously. Isiah was the first modern little man capable of dominating a big man's game. He was quick. He could leap. He could handle the ball like a showman. And he had taught himself to shoot.

As a point guard, he was truly a paradox, both a revolutionary and a throwback all in the same package. The game's other greats—Magic and Oscar—were both tall and played the position like forwards, backing smaller guards down near the basket to score over them. For years, the prototypical point guard was a distributor who looked to pass first.

Isiah, on the other hand, harkened back to the special talents of Bob Cousy and Nate Archibald, when the point guard took 1,300 shots a season and more often than not was the team's number one offensive option. Instead of passing, this rare breed looked to score.

For years, the pro basketball mindset was fixed on the tall point guard as the ideal. Every NBA general manager seemed to be looking for another Magic. But time proved that Magic was a unique package, a big man with the fluid moves of a guard. Even the most athletic big guards simply couldn't deliver what he did, when he did.

Quite suddenly, there was Isiah, proving all over again that the athletic little man could find a path to success through a land of giants. Soon, NBA teams were going for little big men. And a host of them followed. Kevin Johnson. Terry Porter. John Stockton. Mark Price. Derek Harper. Pooh Richardson. Sherman Douglas.

"I guess I was ahead of my time," Isiah said with satisfaction.

Yet, as much as style and talent, it was his mental approach to the game that set him apart. Other players have strongly desired to win an NBA championship, but Thomas swas wholly consumed by the notion. He spent hours studying the people who won world championships,

Thomas came back from wrist surgery in April 1991 to lead the Pisotns past the Hawks in the playoffs.

particularly his friend, Magic. Thomas wanted to know what they knew. He revered winners. Larry Bird. Magic. Pat Riley. K.C. Jones. He wanted to be like them. He flattered them. Cajoled them. He wanted to duplicate their success. Whatever he could steal, he stole. The mannerisms were the easy part. Getting inside their minds was the real challenge. He wanted to think like an NBA champion.

He would pick Magic's brain in late-night phone calls to the West Coast. They would spend hours talking about what it took to win a championship. "I hate that I taught him," Magic would say later. "That's the only thing. I should go back and kick myself."

For the most part, it was only knowledge. The real wisdom Isiah would have to earn himself. The hard way. Which he gladly did, pushing himself and his teammates, night in and night out.

Why did Isiah Thomas want to win championships so badly? Some observers have concluded that his drive came from his meager

The Thomas spirit.

The fan favorite.

He charged the Pistons in '88.

... until he was derailed in the Finals against Los Angeles.

He has always played the mind game.

beginnings in a Chicago ghetto. Many youngsters have come out of the inner city playing basketball, yet few have driven themselves to the point of exhaustion to win championships. Thomas had first shown this singular desire at the University of Indiana, where as a sophomore he had led the Hoosiers to the NCAA title.

After that championship season he declared hardship status and entered the 1981 draft, and the Pistons made him the second overall pick in the field. He really didn't have to prove anything. He was a bright young guard who showed offensive brilliance. But he was only 6'1", and Detroit was a terrible team. Nobody really expected him to be dominant. He could have had a lot of fun and made great money just being Isiah, the kid with the million-dollar smile.

But he wanted to be more than that. He wanted to be bathed in that ineffable light of joy reserved for champions.

So he did what Pat Riley and Magic and Larry Bird and Bill Russell had done.

He played the mind game.

"And that," like the poet once said, "has made all the difference."

Thomas single-handedly delivered a win in Game One of the 1990 Finals.

He battled the Bulls on a broken foot in the '91 Eastern Conference Finals.

The Troy, N.Y., YMCA team in 1901, which became the Troy Trojans.

Detroit Eagles coach Dutch Dehnert.

Dr. James Naismith.

"Making The Ball Sing:"
Pro Basketball's Early Years

EDITOR'S NOTE:

In celebration of the centennial of basketball (James Naismith invented the game in December 1891), THE PISTONS' YEARBOOK includes the following retrospective of pro basketball's early years.

From its beginnings in 1896, professional basketball sported a fearlessness. Its ranks were populated by a competitive, hard-driving breed of men who weren't deterred by the Victorian notion that "professionalism" in athletics was somehow ungentlemenly, even dishonorable.

Naismith had invented the game at the YMCA's International Training School in Springfield, Massachusetts (which would later become Springfield College). Through YMCAs, the game quickly spread around the world.

Professionalism in all sports was a major concern in the 1890s, and the YMCA immediately sought to limit and contain professional basketball.

Dr. Luther Gulick, a YMCA official, wrote in 1898 that "when men commence to make money out of sport it degenerates with tremendous speed. It has inevitably resulted in men of lower character going into the game."

While money was a motivation for the early pros, it wasn't the force that drove them. Basketball was too risky a venture for that. Most who played and promoted it needed day jobs to get by. Intensity, rather than greed,

The sport spread rapidly, and before long, a pro could make good money by playing for one or more teams several nights a week.

seemed to be the characteristic they shared. Many had begun playing the game on YMCA teams and become quite good at it. The better they played, the more they wanted to play. This, in turn, precipitated inevitable conflicts with YMCA officials over the use of the gym. Basketballers wanted to play all the time. And when the YMCA said no, the players went elsewhere. To local armories or Masonic Temples or hotel ballrooms. Anyplace would do, just so long as it had a high ceiling and decent lighting.

The sport spread rapidly, and before long, a pro could make good money by playing for one or more teams several nights a week. Within a few decades, certain stars could pull down $2,400 a year, about three times the earnings of the average laborer. Despite this, the pro game remained a stepchild as leagues and franchises sprang to life across the Northeast, fluttered briefly, then died. The surviving teams were mostly barnstormers who traveled about the country playing the locals. These early pros saw basketball as it was played in every region, and they incorporated the best ideas into their styles. They developed quick, short

passing offenses and ran them off the post, an innovation that quickly found its way to the college game. Joe Lapchick, an early pro who later coached St. John's and the New York Knickerbockers, described this snappy passing style as "making the ball sing."

This whirring of the old laced balls was the pro's anthem, and they were proud of it. It was the song, not the money, they played for. They wanted to hear it each night. So they rode the trains to face hostile crowds in cold, gaslit gyms. Afterward, they drank a few beers and went on to the next town. What they were searching for, they weren't exactly sure. But in the end they found it.

It was the sport's future.

THE CAGERS

There have been claims that professional basketball began in Herkimer, New York, in 1893, but most historians agree that Trenton, New Jersey, in 1896 was the birthplace of the pro game.

The Trenton Basketball Team was the offspring of a successful Trenton YMCA team that had beaten other YMCA and college clubs around New York and Philadelphia during 1895-96. Based on their success, the Trenton players declared themselves national champions and entertained thoughts of greater conquests.

But trouble apparently arose between the team members and the YMCA secretary, which led to the players forming a professional team

Heerdt   Burkhardt (Phy. Dir.)   Maier   Miller

Rohde   Faust

GERMAN Y. M. C. A., BUFFALO, N. Y.

The Buffalo Germans, 1904 "world champions."

Outfitted in velvet shorts and long tights, Trenton played its first "pro" game on Saturday, November 7, 1896, at the Masonic Temple. Seats sold for 25 cents, standing room for 15 cents.

and playing their home games at the local Masonic Temple. The stars, captain Fred Cooper and Albert Bratton, set up a 10-man roster and scheduled 20 games against YMCA, high school and college teams.

Outfitted in velvet shorts and long tights, Trenton played its first "pro" game on Saturday, November 7, 1896, at the Masonic Temple. Seats sold for 25 cents, standing room for 15 cents. The opponent was the Brooklyn YMCA, billed in promotions as the champions of New York. The event drew a crowd of 700, who saw Trenton win, 16-1, with Brooklyn's sole point coming on a late free throw. Seven men played to a side, and Cooper led the scoring with six points. The team's 10 players reportedly pocketed $15 each from gate receipts, but historian Robert W. Peterson in his excellent book, Cages To Jumpshots, has discounted that. Based on gate receipts, the players probably earned about $5 each, Peterson figured. Regardless, the pro game was alive. Trenton went on to post a 19-1 record for the 1896-97 season, their sole loss coming to Millville, New Jersey, a team they later beat. Cooper, an English immigrant who had played soccer, helped the team fashion a slick passing game, which made Trenton quite popular, even with the fans of opposing teams.

The team manager, Fred Padderatz, a carpenter, strung chicken wire around the Masonic Temple court to keep the ball in play. Before long, this wire "cage" came to be a prominent feature of early pro basketball. Reportedly, Padderatz did this in response to an editorial comment in the Trenton Daily True American that "the fellows play like monkeys and should be put in a cage."

However, there was a more practical reason. The "cage" prevented the ball from leaving play. Under the early rules, whoever retrieved the ball after it went out of bounds was allowed to put it into play, which resulted in fearsome struggles out of bounds for the ball. In many smaller gyms of the era, the teams simply played the walls as boundaries and allowed the ball to bounce back into continuous play. Often passes and shots would be angled off the walls. But larger venues presented problems with the out-of-bounds scramble. This was a particular nuisance for pro teams with paying customers.

Padderatz's innovation wasn't adopted immediately by other teams, but within a few seasons it came to be the standard for professional games. High school and college teams apparently never used cages. From Padderatz's chicken wire there developed a system of rope and wire cages draped about the court, some strung 15 to 20 feet high for keeping the ball in play. Thus basketball came to be known as the "cage game" and its players the "cagers."

The cage frequently resulted in wicked injuries and burns as players hurled themselves against it going after loose balls. Fans were said to be fond of poking nitting needles, lighted cigarettes and other prods at the players through the netting. In some Pennsylvania mining towns, spectators took to heating nails and tossing them over the cages onto opponents shooting free throws. But that's getting a bit ahead of the story.

Soon other YMCA teams sought to match Trenton's success, which brought the rapid spread of "professional" teams throughout New England, New York, Pennsylvania and New Jersey. In New York, the 23rd Street YMCA team won the first national AAU tournament, and its members decided to turn pro, which meant they lost their YMCA affiliation. So they named themselves the Wanderers and spent their weekends traveling about the region on trains to play games, for which they usually earned $12 to $15 per player. Although the Original Celtics have been credited with developing post play, the Wanderers also devised an early version in which a player would stand with the ball at the foul line with his back to the basket, ready to pass to a cutting teammate. By 1901, the Wanderers had picked up what may have been basketball's first endorsement contract when each player received $5 to boost Hood's Laboratories spring tonic water.

THE NATIONAL LEAGUE

Unlike the college game, which didn't allow players to take more than a one-bounce dribble, early pro rules allowed players to take a series of two-handed, single-bounce dribbles. As a result, the game kept football's rough nature, with broad, hulking men dominating the ball up and down the floor, forcing their way near the goal to score. Head-on collisions were numerous, particularly in the small gyms of the era, many of which presented other obstacles, such as hot stoves, steam pipes and even posts in the middle of the floor supporting the roof. (Legend has it that the posts in middle of the Trenton YMCA floor led the original idea of "post" play.) For the 1897-98 season, the number of players in pro games was reduced from seven to five per side, helping to ease the sport's crowded feel.

The early players had no contracts or guarantees. Some were paid per game, while others simply split the leftovers of the gate. Alarmed at the pro game's growing numbers, Amatuer Athletic Union officials at first attempted to prevent YMCA teams from playing games against pros, but they relented in 1899, allowing games so long as the pro players were registered with the AAU as pros.

In 1898, a group of New Jersey sports editors founded the National Basketball League with six franchises, including Trenton, Camden, Millville and three in or near Philadelphia. Each team was required to install a cage around its home floor; court size was specified at 65 x 35 feet. The hoop was set a dozen

An early Spalding equipment ad.

inches out from wire backboards, 4 x 4 feet. The league's four referees earned $4 per game, while the players earned $3.75 for playing two games per week.

Play began in December, and by January three teams had folded. Their remains were shaped into a fourth club in Philadelphia and the National League chugged on. Trenton won the first two championships, and in the third year the Wanderers joined the league and claimed the title. Several other leagues—the American, the Interstate and a New England circuit—all began play at the turn of the century, then quickly folded as the teams competed for stars.

The National League folded in December 1903 but not before producing what some consider to be

the first jump-shooter, Jack "Snake" Deal of Camden.

Other early stars of the pro game included:

• Edward A. Wachter, who began playing YMCA ball in 1896 in Troy, New York and graduated to a pro career that included more than 1,800 games. He followed that up with more than 20 years of coaching, including a stint at Harvard.

• Barney Sedran, who was just 5'4" and considered too small for his high school team but later starred for CCNY. Whereas most early pros went into the game right out of high school, Sedran was one of the first to come from college. An early master of the set shot, he played on 10 championship teams in 15 years, including the Troy Trojans, the Cleveland Rosenblums, the Fort

Wayne Knights of Columbus and the Carbondale Salukis (who won 35 straight in 1914-15). Sedran later became a pro coach.

• Bill Cummer, of Connellsville, Pennsylvania, who led the Central League in 1911-12 with 1,404 points in 62 games (a remarkable 23-point average, about as many points as most teams scored). As the team's designated free-throw shooter, he made 938 of his points on free throws. Pro teams abandoned the designated free-throw shooter in 1915, while the colleges persisted in the rule until 1924.

• Dutch Wohlfarth, of Johnstown, Pennsylvania, who was known as the "blind dribbler" because he could bounce the ball without looking at it, which was considered quite a feat in the early game.

• Thomas Barlow, who played pro ball from 1912 to 1932 with numerous Eastern League teams. Among the first pro players to appear in Madison Square Garden, Barlow's presence was billed as "Caveman Barlow Here Tonight."

THE GERMANS VS. BASLOE

Like Trenton and the Wanderers, the Buffalo Germans began life as an amateur YMCA team, organizing in 1895 when the players were 14 years old. They represented the German YMCA in Buffalo and were managed by Fred Burkhardt, the YMCA's physical director. Over 29 seasons, nine of them amateur, they won 761 games and lost 85.

In 1901, the Germans whipped Hobart College 134-0. Also that summer, the city of Buffalo hosted the Pan American Exposition, an array of cultural festivities which included an AAU basketball tournament. The games were 20 minutes long and played outdoors on grass courts. To keep their footing, the players wore cleats. The Germans, a well-oiled hoops machine, easily won this competition and trumpeted themselves as world champions in their barnstorming travels about the region. Then in the summer of 1904, they won a series of exhibition games held in conjunction with the Olympic Games at the St. Louis World's Fair, thus furthering their claims of world championship.

For the 1904-05 season, the Germans, led by team captain Allie Heerdt, began touring as professionals. They did this for the next 20 seasons, although they seldom traveled far from their home region. Most were employed in Buffalo and could not afford to leave their jobs. Among their victims, the Germans listed the Carlisle Indians and Jim Thorpe.

Between 1908 and 1911, the Germans won 111 straight games, outscoring their opponents by an average of 54-18. They were known for running up scores, beating teams by margins of 90 points or more. Most of their 111 consecutive wins were against amateur teams in and around Buffalo. During the streak, the Germans apparently played no games against pro teams from the stronger leagues. In 1908, before the streak began, they were routed in a double-header by a Gloversville, New York, team led by Hall of Famer Ed Wachter.

Frank Basloe, a colorful promoter out of Herkimer, New York, managed the team that finally ended the Buffalo streak in a sold-out armory in Mohawk, New York. Before 2,800 fans, Basloe's 31st Separate Company team won, 18-16 or 26-21, according to conflicting reports. But the Germans returned the favor, 30-18, in Buffalo two weeks later.

Basloe had been managing pro teams since 1903, when at age 16, he created a letterhead declaring "Herkimer—Champions of the Mohawk Valley." After scheduling nine road games in 1903, he decided to find players for his team. His recruits, including Ed Wachter's brother Lew, agreed to play for $5 per game. Basloe then borrowed $10 from his mother to pay his team's train fare to the first of the nine games in Ogdensburg, New York. When the tour was over, Basloe had turned his bluff into nearly a $300 profit.

His rivalry with the Germans didn't end with the 1911 game. During the 1913-14 season, Basloe reorganized the Oswego (New York) Indians to make them more competitive with the Germans. Among his changes, he brought in legendary playmaker Oscar "Swede" Grimstead. The Indians won a double-header with the Germans, while the two teams disputed the score of a third game. The next season, 1914-15, the Indians posted a 121-6 record, including wins in three out of four games with Buffalo.

Except for a pause during World War I, Basloe's teams—known alternately as the 31st Separate Company of Herkimer, the Oswego Indians, and the Basloe Globetrotters—played every season from 1903 to 1923, traveling nearly 100,000 miles each year. They won 1,327 games and lost 121.

In 1931, the original Germans, then 51 years old, got back together to play a younger local team. Proving that old pros were as tough as they claimed, the Germans won by a point.

Another great team of the era was the Troy Trojans, led by 6'6" Ed Wachter and his brother Lew (manager and player). Between 1901 and 1912, the Trojans won four straight titles in various leagues. They, too, were known for teamwork and a smart passing game. For 1914-15, they barnstormed through the Midwest and North Dakota and won 29 straight games.

WHIRLWINDS AND CELTICS

The Original Celtics sent pro basketball off to a new style and pace in the 1920s. They were fancy and good, and they brought the pro game its first national attention.

Frank McCormack formed the

team as the New York Celtics in 1914 with teenage players from Manhattan's West Side. Beginning competition as semipros during the 1916-17 season, they played home games at the Amsterdam Opera House on West 44th Street and posted a 33-10-1 record. Then World War I brought an end to their organization.

James Furey, a promoter, tried to take over the name after the armistice, but McCormack refused to give up the rights to it. So Furey named his group the Original Celtics. Of the New York Celtics, Furey kept players Pete Barry and John Whitty, and to them he added a collection of veteran pros, including Swede Grimstead, the Oswego Indians ballhandler; Johnny Beckman, a 5'8" forward who could score; and 5'11" Dutch Dennert, a star guard. They racked up a 65-4 record for 1918-19 and packed as many as 4,000 into their home court, the Central Opera House.

The other big pro team at that time was the New York Whirlwinds, featuring Barney Sedran, Nat Holman and Max Friedman. In 1921, the Whirlwinds and Celtics met in a series for the championship of New York. The first game at the 71st Regiment Armory drew 11,000 fans, then the largest crowd ever to see a basketball game in America. That first game was played under amateur rules, which resulted in more than 50 fouls. With Holman canning 22 free throws, the Whirlwinds won, 40-27. The Celtics then claimed the second game, 26-24, at the 69th Regiment Armory. The third game in the series was never played, apparently because gamblers attempted to have the outcome fixed.

Holman and Chris Leonard of the Whirlwinds joined the Celtics for the next season, 1921-22, along with 6'4" George "Horse" Haggerty. Jim Furey began promoting this combined team as "national champions." At mid season, the Celtics joined the Eastern League and later won the title that spring. When the league struggled at the outset of the 1922-23 season, the Celtics switched to the Metropolitan

Allie Heerdt of the Buffalo Germans.

League only to find the financial prospects just as dismal. Furey's solution was to take his team barnstorming through a 205-game schedule. They finished 193-11-1. Ties were unusual in basketball, but reportedly the Celtics had a practice of asking for more money when a game went to overtime. If the local promoter refused, the game was called a tie.

To keep the team together, Furey gave the players exclusive contracts for as much as $10,000. To bolster the roster, he added 6'5" Joe Lapchick, a veteran pro center who

had played for numerous teams since he was 19. For the next three seasons, the Celtics traveled about the Northeast, Midwest and South, playing as many as 140 games a year. In Chattanooga, Tennessee, on one of these forays, Dutch Dennert supposedly created the post play. Many teams of that era used a "standing guard" set in the lane to interfere with their opponents' offensive maneuvers. According to legend, Dennert stood at the foul line with his back to the standing guard and passed off to his teammates cutting to the basket. Certainly,

The Carbondale, Pa., team won 35 straight in 1914-15.

Dennert and the Celtics popularized the move, but Holman himself often pointed out that post-type passing strategies had been in use well before Dennert employed them.

The Celtics also are credited with developing zone and switching man-to-man defenses. And Holman, who was a showman of a passer, became a master at drawing fouls by exaggerating contact with a defensive player, a ploy that Bill Laimbeer has elevated to an art form. Most important, the Celtics carried the message of pro basketball across the regions, and in the process they learned new tricks at every stop. When the pro game stepped up with a new nationwide league in 1925, Furey's team was ready to come off the barnstorming trail.

THE AMERICAN LEAGUE

The old style eastern pro game, with its cages and double dribbles, began dying in the 1920s. The various leagues struggled with players jumping from team to team. The fans lost interest, and the leagues folded. Meanwhile, pro basketball in the Midwest—Cleveland, Fort Wayne, Chicago—enjoyed relative success, sometimes playing before as many as 10,000 spectators. This "western" pro game was played under college rules and had more to offer than the eastern game, where the fans had to peer through the netting to see thickly built men bully their way upcourt with the double dribble.

In tune with these changes, the American Basketball League was formed for the 1925-26 season.

Cages were outlawed, and backboards were required. The league's rules were heavily influenced by the AAU game. Of special importance was the adoption of the standard dribble, which opened the door to more college stars, and in turn, helped build the pro sport's popularity.

The ABL was the first truly national league, with nine franchises in Detroit, Cleveland, Washington, Boston, Brooklyn, Rochester, Buffalo, Chicago and Fort Wayne. Like pro baseball and football in that era of limited travel, pro basketball didn't venture into the far West. Instead, the western United States was caught up in AAU competition. The national AAU tournament, held in Kansas City, regularly drew 9,000 fans.

The ABL officials hoped to mirror the success of the college game and

The early New York Celtics.

the western game. The league's president was Joseph Carr, who also served as the National Football League's president. The ABL's prime organizers were Chicago Bears owner George Halas; Washington businessman George Preston Marshall, who later owned the Washington Redskins; and Max Rosemblum, who owned a department store and named his team the Cleveland Rosenblums.

The Boston Whirlwinds folded during the season, but the remaining eight teams pushed on. (The Detroit Pulaski Post finished 2-12.) That spring, the league's best-of-five championship series, promoted as Basketball's World Series, featured the Brooklyn Arcadians, winners of the first half of the schedule, against the Cleveland Rosenblums, winners of the second half. An estimated 10,000 fans filled Cleveland's Public Auditorium for each of the first two

games, as Honey Russell and Marty Friedman led the Rosenblums to a 2-0 lead in games. Game three in New York's 71st Regiment Armory drew only 2,000, and Cleveland swept the series with a 23-22 win. The Original Celtics had been invited to join the league that first season but declined. Once Cleveland won the championship, Celtics manager Jim Furey challenged the winners to a series. But Rosenblum turned the offer down.

For its second season, the ABL reshuffled. The Buffalo Bisons (run by Allie Heerdt of Germans fame) folded. So Carr added the Philadelphia Warriors (run by Eddie Gottlieb) and the Baltimore Orioles to bring the league back to 10 teams. The 1926-27 scheduled 42 games for each team, but Detroit (the Pulaski Post had changed its name to the Detroit Cardinals) and Brooklyn both dropped out in December.

The Celtics then took over the Brooklyn franchise and joined the league. Furey, meanwhile, had been charged with embezzling $187,000 from the department store where he worked as head cashier. The Celtics' manager was convicted and sentenced to Sing Sing for three years, making the ABL a likely refuge for a team without a manager. Although they took over Brooklyn's 0-5 record, the Celtics rapidly moved to the top of the league. Holman, Joe Lapchick, Chris Leonard, Pete Barry and Dutch Dennert had played hundreds of games together over the previous five years and rolled over the ABL opposition. They soon added forward Davey Banks and became even more formidable. The Celtics won the second half of the schedule, then swept the Rosenblums in the World Series with a dazzling display of the short passing game.

But the league's second season

also brought rumblings of financial trouble. Attendance was sluggish. Despite the AAU rules, play remained rough. As a solution, the ABL decided to disqualify players after five fouls in a game (the colleges disqualified after four), a change protested by many old pros. A new rule also prohibited the player with the ball from staying in the foul lane longer than three seconds.

Another curse was lopsided games, which brought complaints that the Celtics were too good for the rest of the league. Although they seldom ran up scores, the Celtics confirmed their superiority over the 1927-28 season by rolling up a 40-9 record and whipping the Fort Wayne Hoosiers in the championship series, 3-1. Their success brought cries for the league to break up the franchise, but the ABL didn't have to. Bad management took care of the job. With Furey in prison, the club was in disarray. The Original Celtics Exhibition Corporation was shut down and the players dispersed to other teams. Lapchick, Dennert and Barry went to the Rosenblums. Holman and Banks became the property of a new team, the New York Hakoahs.

The talent-rich Cleveland Rosenblums closed the 1928-29 season with a four-game sweep of the Hoosiers in the championship series, and each member of the winning team earned $500. The losers picked up $380. But the good times and fat paychecks were short-lived. The stock market crashed as the next season opened, and with the economic hardship came challenges from other leagues. The Eastern League had revived itself, plus a new National Basketball League operated in Ohio and Michigan.

Still, the ABL played on. The 1929-30 season found eight teams playing 54-game schedules. The lineup included a retooled edition of the Celtics, made possible by Furey's parole. Dennert, Lapchick and Barry remained with the Rosenblums. Holman and Banks returned to the Celtics, but the franchise again folded in December. In the playoffs that spring of 1930, the Rosenblums

swept the Rochester Centrals, 4-0, but even the crowds in Cleveland were relatively puny, about 3,000.

Hoping that it could capture some of the college game's popularity, the league required for 1930-31 that each team play two rookies. But the times weren't right for the ABL. Max Rosenblum folded his championship franchise that December, telling the Cleveland News that fans "are disinterested in professional basketball." Still, the league struggled on, with the Fort Wayne Hoosiers beating the Brooklyn Visitations, 4-2, for the 1931 championship. One game in Brooklyn was broadcast by radio in Fort Wayne, which, according to historian Robert Peterson, may

Still, the ABL played on. The 1929-30 season found eight teams playing 54-game schedules. The lineup inluded a retooled edition of the Celtics, made possible by Furey's parole.

have been a first for pro basketball.

The ABL officially succumbed in November 1931, as the Depression worsened, but commissioner John J. O'Brien reorganized it in 1933-34, and it survived as an eastern regional circuit until 1953. However, it was never again a "national" league.

With the decline of the ABL, many pro teams returned to the heavy barnstorming schedules that had been profitable in earlier times. Seeking to recapture their glory, the Celtics reunited in 1931 and set out for another round of travels in their seven-passenger Pierce-Arrow. Age had caught up with them, and they were no longer the dominant team in basketball. Still, they drew crowds in small towns around the country, often playing before high school players and coaches eager to watch the slick passing game at work. One by one, the older players began to retire. Lapchick and Holman had continued to play while coaching college

basketball, but their coaching duties began to take more of their time. In 1935, singer Kate Smith became the Celtics' sponsor. Soon the only old face left was Pete Barry, who became the coach. The Kate Smith Celtics, which competed for a time in the ABL, played their games at the Hippodrome, a Manhattan theater. The floor was on a stage, presaging the era when basketball would become entertainment. But the Kate Smith Celtics were never as dominant at the Originals. Regardless, the Celtics name came to stand for excellence, a tradition that would be revived in Boston some years after the Originals had closed up shop.

THE RENS

Perhaps the best pro team of the 1930s was the Renaissance Big Five from Harlem. Known as the Rens, this club stacked up 2,318 wins against 381 losses over 26 seasons. Like the Celtics, they were barnstormers who relied on the passing game and a stifling defense. But there was one big difference between the clubs—the Rens were black.

There was no Negro pro basketball league during the era, so African-Americans had to travel a narrow path to success. They had to be good enough to draw crowds and smart enough to avoid the Jim Crow troubles that plagued the country. The Rens were able to do both. In 1932-33, they toured the deep South and pulled it off handily. Just about everywhere they traveled, even across the Northeast and Midwest, they encountered the meanness of segregation. But the Rens always got their money before they played, and they practiced a brand of clean, exciting basketball that opened many closed minds.

Honey Russell once described the Rens as "one of the cleanest teams I ever played against. They just played basketball that was so good they didn't have to resort to any kind of rough stuff."

Robert Douglas, an immigrant from the West Indies who played ball in

Harlem, founded the club in 1923. He wanted to call them the Spartans, but he needed sponsorship. The Renaissance Casino in Harlem agreed to provide a home in its ballroom, so they became the Renaissance Big Five.

They gained notoriety in the mid 1920s during a series of games with the Celtics. Over three seasons, they met the Celtics nine times and won four of them. The Rens also beat every major ABL team they faced. By the 1930s, they were playing 130 games a year and winning just about all of them. Their big men were Wee Willie Smith at 6'5" and Charles "Tarzan" Cooper at 6'3"; the rest of the roster was 6 feet or less. Clarence "Fat" Jenkins and Bill Yancey also played baseball in the Negro leagues.

The 1932-33 team rolled up an 88-game winning streak on its way to a 120-8 record. They played the aging Celtics 14 times that season and won eight, but the Celtics ended their winning streak.

Even at the height of their success, the Rens had to endure the discomfort of segregation. Many hotels and restaurants refused them service, so they often ate coldcuts and arranged to stay in private homes. Many nights they had to drive extra miles to find a place to sleep. Their road secretary carried a pistol just in case of trouble, and sometimes there were tense moments. But Douglas paid them well and kept them together, which meant they just got better with time.

"We loved being the Renaissance," Hall of Famer Pop Gates told Peterson, "because we thought we were the best, and we were happy and proud to represent the Negro people and give them something they could be proud of and adhere to."

In 1939, the Chicago Herald-American began sponsorship of a pro tourney that ran for the next decade. Played in Chicago Stadium, the tournament drew 12 to 16 teams each year from the various league champions and top barnstorming teams. In some years the crowds reached 20,000, and the pro players

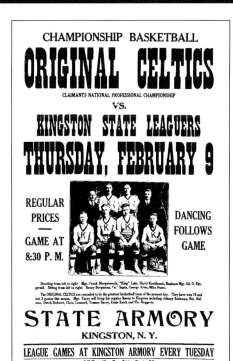

considered it the event that settled their championship. The Rens, led by Pop Gates, then a 21-year-old rookie, ran through the 1939 tournament field, beating the Osh-Kosh All Stars, champions of the National Basketball League, 34-25, for the world championship.

World War II soon put a brake on the nation's barnstorming acts, causing Douglas to shut down the Rens for a time. But Cooper, Smith and several other Rens played as the Washington Bears and again won the Chicago tournament in 1943. They regrouped after the war and played during 1948-49 as the Dayton Rens in the National Basketball League, one of the early developments in breaking pro basketball's color line.

John Wooden, UCLA's great coach, played against the Rens several times in the late '30s as a member of the Indianapolis Kautsky Grocers. He called them "the best I ever saw."

GOTTLIEB AND THE SPHAS

Depending on whom you talk to, Eddie Gottlieb is remembered as either the "father of pro basketball," or the world's biggest tightwad. He probably couldn't have been one without being the other in the pro

game's lean early years. Promoter. Coach. Owner. Entrepreneur. All of those tags fit Gottlieb.

Since 1918, shortly after he graduated from South Philadelphia High School, he had been infatuated with basketball as a business. Back then, he and a group of his young Jewish buddies had formed a team, and Gottlieb talked the Young Men's Hebrew Association into sponsoring it. Three years later, the association withdrew its sponsorship, and Gottlieb moved the team to the South Philaelphia Hebrew Association. They drew their name, the SPHAs, from the sponsor's acronym on their jerseys in Hebrew letters. It wasn't long before the second association dropped its sponsorship, but the SPHAs kept the name anyway.

During the game's formative years, as many as half of all pro players were Jewish, but the SPHAs were the best-known team with a roster made up almost entirely of Jews.

Gottlieb signed up Davey Banks, a shooter from New York, and Charley Tettemer from Trentron, and by the mid 1920s the SPHAs were arguably one of the best teams in pro basketball. When the ABL started in 1925-26, the SPHAs (playing as the Philadelphia Hebrews) beat five of the league's six teams in exhibition games (they lost to the Rosenblums). Gottlieb then scheduled best-of-three series with both the Celtics and the Rens, and he added veteran players Stretch Meehan and Tom Barlow. With that added firepower, the SPHAs took the Celtics series in three games and swept the Rens, 36-33, and 40-39.

The victories were still fresh when the Celtics signed Banks away. The SPHAs slipped further when Gottlieb agreed to manage the Philadelphia Warriors in the ABL. When the American League began struggling in 1928, Gottlieb rejuvenated his SPHAs with college stars, such as Moe Goldman of CCNY and Harry Litwack of Temple. Competing in the old Eastern League, they won three championships, then later moved into the scaled-down, regional version of the American League. The SPHAs

The Original Celtics, left to right, Joe Lapchick, Chris Leonard, "Dutch" Dehnert, Pete Barry, Nat Holman, John Whitty, John Beckman, and Eddie Burke.

also continued to barnstorm on the side, with Gottlieb working out deals and promotions.

While running his team, Gottlieb grew up with the pro game. He nurtured it through the days of two-handed dribbles and center jumps after every bucket. As time went on, he figured ways to promote it and even make a little money from it. As his players used to say, "Gotty" had a knack for counting the house. From the bench, he could scan the stands and figure whether the draw was 500, 800 or 1,000. In time, there was nobody who knew more about promoting basketball than Eddie Gottlieb. Like other promoters, Gottlieb found he could attract a decent crowd if he combined the games with a dance afterward, the only problem being that usually the "fans" were more interested in the dance. It wasn't unusual to have girls in heels interrupt play with an inadvertent stroll across the floor.

Back then, the game was played in three periods. Gottlieb's boys would play a period, then the fans would dance a while. Then they'd play another period. Some nights former Temple star Gil Fitch would exchange his SPHAs uniform for a tux and lead his band.

The SPHAs played most of their games at Philly's old Broadwood Hotel, a nightspot for Jewish singles. "The floor was slick, a lot of dance wax on it," recalled Robert "Jake" Embry, owner of the Baltimore Bullets. "The players were used to sliding and shooting. They'd dribble, slide about five feet and shoot."

Even as they barnstormed, the SPHAs dominated the scaled-down version of the American League, winning seven championships in the 15 years the league operated. In 1946, Gottlieb managed and coached the Philadelphia Warriors in the Basketball Association of America, the forerunner of the NBA, and the SPHAs struggled along on their own. For a time, they barnstormed with the Rens and are believed to be the only team to ever beat the Rens at the Renaissance Casino.

Each year at Christmas, Gottlieb would take the SPHAs on a western tour, through Harrisburg, Pennsylvania, then on to Akron, Cleveland and Oshkosh, Wisconsin. The players, who made $100 for the tour, often asked Gottlieb why they simply couldn't take the week off. "Because," he replied, "you are pioneers for a big league someday."

THE GLOBETROTTERS

The Harlem Globetrotters got their start in Chicago in 1927, but they were merely a regional team then. It would take more than a decade before they began to garner "global" attention.

They began existence as the Savoy Big Five, playing out of Chicago's Savoy Ballroom. In 1926, they encountered a portly 23-year-old promoter, Abe Saperstein, from Chicago's north side. He began booking the team and within months took over its management. In January

Meadow Lemon, a boy growing up in Wilmington, North Carolina, saw a newsreel on the 'Trotters in the late 1940s and described it this way: "I could hardly stay in my seat with that jumpin', jivin', whistlin', music blaring. It made you want to dance, and that's what these guys, these Harlem Globetrotters were doing."

1927, he dubbed them Saperstein's New York and booked them for a game in nearby Hinckley, Illinois. None of the players was from New York, but the name sounded worldly to Saperstein. Later they would become just plain "New York" and later "Saperstein's Harlem New York." After about eight years or so they became the Harlem Globe Trotters. Saperstein settled on that because Harlem identified the players as black, and Globe Trotters suggested world travel.

In later years, they would become known for their humorous routines and slick ball-handling, often performed to the accompaniment of "Sweet Georgia Brown." But in the early days, the Globetrotters played their basketball straight. They did, however, apparently have their warm-up "circle" in their early days. Over the years, this "circle" evolved into the world's classiest ball-handling routine. The entertainment and humor were said to be a means of deflecting the ugly racial moods the team sometimes encountered on the road. Plus, if the local teams had fun and the crowd laughed, people didn't mind losing, and the Globetrotters were often invited back.

They played some of the great barnstorming teams during the 1930s, but hadn't traveled very far from Chicago. In fact, they hadn't even played in Harlem. Their breakthrough came with the 1939 season when they stacked up a 148-13 record, good enough for an invitation to the Chicago tournament.

James "Pappy" Ricks (right) helped make the Rens the best of their era.

The Globetrotters lost a close game to the Rens, but that showed how good they were. For 1940, the 'Trotters (with Bernie Price, Babe Pressley, Sonny Boswell, Hillery Brown, and Inman Jackson) won the tournament, beating the NBL's Chicago Bruins (owned by George Halas), 31-29, in overtime. The victory was soon followed by new red-white-and-blue uniforms and a new team bus, and the Globetrotters were on their way.

In the 1940s, Saperstein signed two stars. Reece "Goose" Tatum, a baseball player from Arkansas, had huge hands, long arms and a wonderful wit. And when Oklahoma's Langston University team beat the 'Trotters, Saperstein promptly lured away the star player, Marques Haynes. Building on Tatum's

creativity, the Globetrotters left the straight game to offer fans their hugely entertaining brand of hoops, filled with gimmicks, gags and top-notch ball-handling. But they paused in this conversion long enough to beat George Mikan and the Minneapolis Lakers in exhibition games at Chicago Stadium after World War II (and would play exhibition games against the Lakers through the 1950s).

Meadow Lemon, a boy growing up in Wilmington, North Carolina, saw a newsreel on the 'Trotters in the late 1940s and described it this way: "I could hardly stay in my seat with that jumpin', jivin', whistlin', music blaring. It made you want to dance, and that's what these guys, these Harlem Globetrotters were doing. Smiling, singing, slapping each other on the back, tumbling from the locker room to a basketball court, a big one with thousands of fans in the stands."

Lemon would later become Meadowlark Lemon, Globetrotter star.

The 'Trotters toured Alaska in 1949, then headed for Western Europe and North Africa the next year. In 1951, they toured South and Central America, drawing a crowd of 50,000 in Rio de Janiero. Later that summer, they achieved official "ambassador" status when the U.S. Government asked the 'Trotters to Berlin to help improve relations with Germany after the war. In the same open-air stadium where Adolph Hitler had refused to recognize African-American Olympians 15 years earlier, a crowd of 75,000 showered the Globetrotters with applause. The highlight of the show was the surprise appearance of four-time Olympic gold medalist Jesse Owens, who had been snubbed in 1936.

From there, the 'Trotters fame only spread, and with their return home, they found they were an even bigger attraction in the states. In 1952, they celebrated their 25th anniversary, and later performed their routine for Pope Pius XII.

In 1958, they added center Wilt Chamberlain, who had left the University of Kansas a year early and was waiting to enter the NBA. Even after joining the NBA, Chamberlain spent his summer months touring with the 'Trotters in Europe. In the early 1960s, at the heart of the Cold War, they toured the Soviet Union and met Nikita Khrushchev in Moscow.

In 1961, Saperstein founded the American Basketball League to compete with the NBA, but the venture failed. (During the league's short life, John McClenden coached the Cleveland Pipers, and as such became the first black coach in a professional league.)

Saperstein died in 1966, and in 1967, a group of investors bought the team for $3.7 million. By then the 'Trotters had grown to a network of several touring teams, each spreading the gospel of "Sweet Georgia Brown" across the globe.

As the game of basketball begins its centennial celebration, the 'Trotters will hold their 65th birthday. Without question, they are the longest-running team in the history of the game.

THE NATIONAL LEAGUE

The first strains of the modern pro game appeared in 1935 with the formation of the Midwest Basketball Conference, a loose alliance of semi-pro and industrial teams. The Conference's first two champions were the Chicago Duffy Florals and the Akron Goodyears. In 1937, the alliance became the National Basketball League in hopes it would garner more interest and prestige. A

As the game of basketball begins its centennial celebration, the 'Trotters will hold their 65th birthday. Without question, they are the longest-running team in the history of the game.

dozen years later, the NBA would merge with the Basketball Association of America to form the National Basketball Association.

In the late 1930s, the NBL operated with an array of small-city teams, many of whom took their sponsorship from local businesses. They sported names such as the Toledo Jim White Chevrolets, the Akron Goodyear Winged-foots and the Fort Wayne General Electrics. Some of the sponsoring businesses employed players as workers. Other teams were strictly basketball operations.

The league consisted of 13 franchises (some cost as little as $350) its first season, 1937-38. Each team scheduled its own games, which made for inconsistent competition. But the NBL quickly established a reputation for good players. John Wooden played for the Whiting All-Americans, and the

league's dominant player was 6'4" Leroy "Cowboy" Edwards, who shot the hook with either hand. His team, the Oshkosh All-Stars, lost to the Goodyear Winged-foots in the first championship series, 2-1. Edwards again took his team to the league finals in 1939, but a team sponsored by the Firestone Rubber Company took the championship.

For the 1940 season, the Detroit Eagles and George Halas' Chicago Bruins joined the league. Again it was the Firestones and All-Stars in the championship, with the Firestones winning the third game, 61-60.

Finally in 1941, Edwards and the All-Stars won the championship on their third try. Later that season, the NBL's Detroit Eagles, coached by former Celtic Dutch Dennert, won the Chicago tournament and claimed the world championship.

THE WAR AND INTEGRATION

The bombing of Pearl Harbor in December 1941 had an immediate effect on the pro game. The country mobilized for war, and suddenly the supply of players dried up. To fill the roster of his team, the Toledo Jim White Chevrolets, promoter Sid Goldberg came up with a novel idea—integration. The league's other owners weren't thrilled with the idea, but Goldberg pulled together six whites and four blacks—Zano West, Al Price, Casey Jones and Shannie Barnett—to make a team for the 1942-43 season. This integrated squad lost all four games they played and promptly folded in December.

But the NBL owners still learned something. The integrated teams hadn't brought the fan uproar they had expected. The Chicago Studebakers were also integrated that season, consisting of half Harlem Globetrotters and half white college players. The popularity of the 'Trotters helped the predominantly white crowds accept the change. But the Studebakers broke up before the Chicago tournament when former Loyola of Chicago star Mike Novak had a spat with former Globetrotter Sonny Boswell. Some at first thought the disagreement was

The Detroit Eagles vs. the Harlem Globetrotters in the 1930s.

racial, but the team's players later told historian Robert Peterson that Novak was merely upset because Boswell was shooting too much and passing too little.

There had been instances of integration in pro basketball as early as 1904, when Bucky Lew played with two New England League teams. Historian William F. Himmelman,

known for his extensive research of the early game, has cited other instances:

• Frank "Dido" Wilson played in the Mohawk Valley League in 1907.

• In 1911 and 1917, the Eastern League appears to have included an African-American.

• The 1935 roster of the Buffalo Bisons, a Midwest Basketball

There had been instances of integration in pro basketball as early as 1904, when Bucky Lew played with two New England League teams.

The Globetrotters in Paris in 1950.

Conference team, included 6'4" center Hank Williams.

BIRTH OF THE PISTONS

The Fort Wayne Zollner Pistons joined the NBL in 1941-42 and immediately played their way to the championship game, where they lost to Cowboy Edwards and the All-Stars, 2-1. Hot-shooting guard Bobby McDermott used his fiery competitiveness to drive the Pistons, which survive today as the NBA's Detroit Pistons. The team was founded by Fred Zollner, owner of a piston manufacturing plant.

The Royals were a star-studded cast (Chuck Connors, who would go on to star in the TV series The Rifleman, was a substitute with a penchant for offbeat poetry recitals).

Wartime hardship trimmed the league to five teams for 1942-43, with the rubber company teams, the Goodyears and Firestones, numbering among the casualties. The Sheboygan Redskins beat the

Pistons in the 1943 league championship, but few noticed. The times had gotten harder, and the 1943-44 season found just four teams competing. The Pistons added another fiery guard, Buddy Jeannette, to the backcourt with McDermott, which resulted in Fort Wayne's first championship. They beat the Redskins in the NBL finals, then went on to take the Chicago tournament's world championship.

With the war winding down, the league expanded to six teams in two divisions for 1944-45, but the championship again came down to a Redskins-Pistons battle. Sheboygan took the first two games of the best-of-five series, but the Pistons and McDermott stormed back to claim a second championship. After the season, the league coaches voted McDermott the greatest player in the history of professional basketball.

That little bit of hype helped as the next season opened. McDermott and the Pistons whipped a collection of college all-stars, 63-55, before 23,912 fans at Chicago Stadium. The NBL grew to eight teams with the addition of the Rochester Royals and the Indianapolis Kautskys. The Royals were a star-studded cast (Chuck Connors, who would go on to star in the TV series The Rifleman, was a substitute with a penchant for offbeat poetry recitals). With Bob Davies and Al Cervi in the backcourt and George "Blind Bomber" Glamack, John Mahnken and Fuzzy Levane in the frontcourt, they shoved aside Fort Wayne for the league championship.

The 1946-47 season brought the emergence of the Chicago American-Gears, with 6'10" college star George Mikan out of DePaul. Mikan sat out the early part of the schedule in a contract dispute, then returned. The Pistons, angered by McDermott's thirst for a good fight, traded him to Chicago, where he and Mikan promptly led the Gears to the NBL title.

Even worse for the Pistons, they lost Buddy Jeannette and third guard Chick Reiser to the Baltimore Bullets. It would be years before the franchise would recover.

THE NBA

In 1946, the mood of the country was boom. Economic boom. Housing boom. Baby boom. Entertainment boom. Even, in its own quiet way, a basketball boom.

The end of World War II had brought the return home of hundreds of thousands of G.I.s. And money that had once been directed at the war effort suddenly began flowing into the American economy. First it was a trickle, then a rush, as the nation moved out from the shadow of catastrophe. Sick of war bonds and weapons plants and rationing, people turned their thoughts to rebuilding their lives.

After five years of struggle and sacrifice, the public showed a vast hunger for fun. New products seemed to emerge overnight. Polaroid cameras. 33 1/3 long-playing records. Wash-and-wear shirts. Most fascinating of all was the television set, although there were only about 100,000 tubes (with seven- and twelve-inch screens) in American households and bars in 1946. Even so, programmers were already looking to sports. A Joe Louis fight was aired in June 1946 and by 1947, the World Series would be telecast.

And if things weren't brand new, they were innovative. Suddenly ice cream came in eight flavors, and Americans gobbled up 714 million gallons of it in 1946, apparently much of it by pregnant women.

The biggest product, of course, was babies. Nearly 3.5 million were born in 1946 alone, and the numbers would spiral from there, blowing out all government projections on population. By the 1960s, there would be an extra 30 million Americans, all of them young and eager for excitement.

Looking back, it seems logical that the National Basketball Association, itself a child of this baby boom, would grow and mature with the generation. But back in 1946, starting another pro basketball league seemed like a crazy thing to do. The business climate was as tough as the play on the court. Teams and entire leagues

Bobby McDermott of the Pistons.

struggled through a life-and-death search for cash flow.

Even so, a group of executives gathered in New York in June 1946 to form a new league. They were mostly arena owners and professional hockey managers, and they figured basketball was a good way to keep the buildings busy on off nights. They hoped to bring the charm of the college game to a new pro circuit.

Whereas the National Basketball League had an out-of-the-way setting, the new league began with 11 franchises in major cities. With teams in New York, Boston, Philadelphia, Providence, Toronto, Washington, Chicago, Cleveland, Detroit, Pittsburgh and St. Louis, this new circuit called itself the Basketball Association of America, or the BAA.

The league hustled to begin play that fall of 1946, as newly selected coaches scrambled to find players. Each team set a total salary cap of $55,000, which meant an average annual contract of about $5,000 for the players (some earned $7,500 or higher). With the NBL allowed to pay more, much of the big-name talent remained in the older league. But with

the war ending, there was a surplus of players for both the colleges and the pros.

On November 1, 1946, the New York Knicks beat the Toronto Huskies, 68-66, in the league's first regular-season game. As with the pro leagues that had preceded it, the BAA soon found its share of troubles.

A group of executives gathered in New York in June 1946 to form a new league. They were mostly arena owners and professional hockey managers, and they figured basketball was a good way to keep the buildings busy on off nights.

Franchises opened and closed overnight in those first few years. Before its second season, the new league had lost teams in Detroit, Cleveland, Pittsburgh and Toronto. To replace them, it added Baltimore out of the old American League.

Pro basketball was the learning the same lesson as pro football. Competing leagues meant bidding wars for talent, which meant certain economic failure as operating costs skyrocketed. In 1948, the proud old National Football League had agreed to merge with its upstart rival, the All-America Football Conference. The same fate awaited pro basketball.

Just before the 1948-49 campaign, the four strongest teams in the NBL—Minneapolis, Rochester, Fort Wayne and Indianapolis—left their league to join the BAA's Western Division. The following season, the six surviving teams from the NBL came into the BAA, making for a three-division alignment that was renamed the National Basketball Association.

In no way did the merger mean that the lean times were over. Pro basketball would need time to mature and prosper. But those early years had provided a beginning. And like the rest of the Baby Boom, the NBA was off and toddling.

The Pistons' Mel Hutchins (9), Bob Houbregs (17) and George Yardley (12) watch as George Mikan of the Minneapolis Lakers shoots in 1956.

Zollner And the Ref Who Would Be Coach

The Detroit Pistons are quite proud that they own their own plane, ROUNDBALL ONE. But they weren't the first NBA team to have their own air force. That distinction goes to their Fort Wayne ancestors. In the 1950s, the old Fort Wayne Pistons flew around in team owner Fred Zollner's personal plane, a DC 3, while the rest of the NBA rode trains.

"We'd fly that plane right out of the hangar," recalled Charlie Eckman, a former Piston coach.

As legend has it, Zollner, the owner of a Piston manufacturing plant, was quite eccentric, even bizarre at times. Eckman recalled that the Pistons attempted to fly home from an exhibition game against the Lakers in North Dakota one bad night. A snowstorm apparently blanketed the Midwest, and the low-lying cloud coverage made landing nearly impossible.

The plane circled for some time over Fort Wayne, and the players were concerned about fuel. Zollner grew increasingly irritated with the situation and began stomping on the floor. Finally, the owner got on the plane's radio and attempted to make contact with the devil.

"He said, 'Hello D? This is Z calling,'" Eckman recalled with a chuckle. "He kept calling for the devil, and that scared the shit out of everybody. Lou Eisenstein, a jewish official who was with us, said, 'Mr. Zollner, why don't you talk to Jesus Christ?' Zollner said, 'You don't talk to Jesus Christ on a night like this. The

Charlie Eckman.

devil put this shit up here. He's not doing anything tonight. I'm calling him. 'Hello D. This is Z.' Jocko Collins, the other official traveling with us, was a devout Catholic. He got out his rosary beads and started praying.

"Zollner went back to his seat, and a few minutes later, the captain called back that Fort Wayne had just opened up and we were going in. We landed at 600 feet in a blinding snow and rain storm. Louie Eisenstein kissed the ground when we got out and told Zollner, 'I'll never fly with you again.'"

Retired today and living near his native Baltimore, Eckman finds his memories of Zollner hugely entertaining. It seemed Zollner had girlfriends everywhere, and they were all named Mary, Eckman said. "If she wasn't named Mary, she wasn't his girlfriend. We'd be going to a ball game somewhere, and he'd stop the plane on the way and pick up a Mary.

He'd pick them up in Milwaukee or LaCrosse, wherever there was a Mary.

"He was a goofy bastard," Eckman concluded.

Perhaps the zaniest thing Zollner did was hire Eckman, an NBA ref with no coaching experience, to be his head coach. In fact, Eckman had officiated the previous year's Finals and was considered a solid referee. All the same, he was viewed as somewhat overblown and full of bull. That perspective on him broadened after he went to the bench.

Opposing coaches and players were openly irritated that a mere ref had ascended to a head coaching job. "It was sort of a mockery," Paul Seymour of the Syracuse Nationals said of Eckman's hiring. "Charlie was a real character. He was sort of wimpy, sort of portly, like most of those officials were back then. He was sort of a laugh. I guess at the time Fort Wayne needed a laugh."

The circumstances under which Eckman were hired were certainly laughable. Late in the '53-54 season he had officiated a game in Milwaukee between the Minneapolis Lakers and the Pistons. The Lakers won, and Eckman recalled that afterward in a restaurant, he boastfully told George Mikan, "If I was coaching the Pistons, I'd beat you big clowns."

Eckman, of course, was kidding. But Zollner overheard the comment and remembered it. At the close of the season, he contacted Eckman, flew him to Miami for an interview and

Pistons owner Fred Zollner.

offered him the job.

"I said, 'You got yourself a boy,'" Eckman recalled.

Some had thought Zollner would give the coaching job to Rochester guard Bob Davies or to the Pistons' own veteran guard, Andy Phillip. "People thought Zollner was crazy, that he had gone off his trolley hiring a referee," Eckman said. "All the writers thought he was nuts."

Gifted with an immense capacity for gab, Eckman didn't help matters by constantly pumping out quips about how easy coaching was. But, compared with a referee's life, it was. "It was like a vacation, riding around on a plane and having a suite for a room," Eckman said. "As a referee, you were lucky to get a room. You spent your time riding around from game to game on them trains."

The ref's pay was $50 a game, plus $5 a day meal money and another $5 for incidentals. Saturdays usually meant calling two games. You might call an afternoon game in Philly, then jump on the train for New York to do the second half of a double header. Back then, though, coaching was a penthouse position in the NBA. Zollner offered Eckman a $10,000 contract that first year, which was great money in 1955.

But the biggest difference was the fans. "If you were refereeing, you had no friends," Eckman said. Each town seemed to have a character like the one in Syracuse, whom the officials took to calling the "Strangler," because of his penchant for choking refs. He'd stalk the transgressing official coming off the floor—there never seemed to be proper security, Eckman said—and get the ref in his clutches. "They all knew it," Eckman said, facetiously alleging that Syracuse's management "kept him there for that purpose."

But once Eckman became a coach, the irate fans disappeared and the jeers turned to cheers. "What a feeling!" he said.

In retrospect, he should have kept up a few more pretensions about the difficulty of coaching, Eckman said. "The coaching strategy I made a farce of it, and it didn't sit well with

George Yardley.

some people. But we only had two plays and when we ran them I didn't even know where the ball was. We had no blackboards or papers or lines or Xs or Os or assistant coaches. We had no strategies. The only time pro players make plays is in practice. I was a cheerleader, and I kept everybody happy. It's a simple game."

But there were certain things Eckman had learned as a ref, and it helped him transform Fort Wayne from a third-place finish in the Western Division into an NBA Finals team. Mainly, he gained an understanding of individual matchups. "As a ref, you call 120 games and you get to see who can play who," he

said. "I got to see the whole league. I knew who could play, who went to their right, who went to their left. There's a big difference."

With Eckman coaching, the Pistons ran up a 43-29 record, the best in the Western division. Fort Wayne's success caught opponents off guard. "The guys in the league thought that we'd be a joke, that we'd be cute," Eckman said. "Hell, we out-cuted them."

It helped that Eckman had inherited a talented club, albeit an underachieving one. In the post, he had hulking 6'9" 250-pound Larry Foust, a veteran out of LaSalle, who averaged 17 points and 10 rebounds for 1954-55. Foust had been one of

Piston Bob Houbregs, a Hall of Famer.

made me look like a coach. I told Yardley he was gonna start, and he couldn't thank me enough."

A 6'5" engineer out of Stanford who had played AAU ball, the sophisticated Yardley responded by averaging 17.3 points and nearly 10 rebounds per game. "He was a bald-headed skinny bastard, looked like an insurance man, anything but a basketball player," Eckman said. "But he could play." (Yardley would go on to become the first NBA player to score 2,000 in a season.)

Eckman also had a nice array of bench players to choose from, including Bob Houbregs, Don Meineke, Paul Walther and Dick Rosenthal.

From their first-place regular-season finish, the Pistons met Minneapolis in the Western Finals and finished the Lakers there, 3-1, in a series that included two overtime wins by Fort Wayne. Their victory left the NBA faced with a promoter's nightmare. Fort Wayne vs. Syracuse in the Finals. Two old National Basketball League teams (see "Making The Ball Sing") from two small cities. Both were nice places but hardly media centers. As it was, pro basketball received little media coverage in the 1950s. But the 1955 Finals were even more obscure than usual, which was unfortunate, because the two teams battled through a classic seven-game series to perhaps the most dramatic finish ever.

The series was interesting for Pistons fans for another reason. Two future Pistons coaches, Red Rocha and Earl Lloyd, were well-respected forwards for Syracuse.

The 1955 Finals opened March 31 in Syracuse, where the Pistons took a 75-71 lead midway through the fourth period. But Syracuse came back and won it 86-82 for a 1-0 lead. Foust had scored 26 for Fort Wayne, while Red Rocha led the Nats with 19.

Game Two on April 2 was cut from the same mold, as Syracuse won, 87-84, on a fourth-quarter surge led by Dolph Schayes (the father of current NBA player Danny), who finished with 24. The Nats had led by 11 at half,

the few players over the years capable of giving the Lakers' George Mikan a decent matchup. The solid defensive forward was 6'6" Mel Hutchins, another veteran, out of Brigham Young. The brother of Miss America Colleen Hutchins (who wed Ernie Vandeweghe of the Knicks), Mel averaged 12 points and nearly 10 rebounds a game to go with his excellent defensive play.

The backcourt was veteran as well, with a wealth of playoff experience. First, there was Max Zaslofsky, who had been to the Finals with both Chicago and New York.

Then there was Phillip, one of the Illinois Whiz Kids, who had been to the Finals with Chicago. Also there was Frankie "Flash" Brian, who scored at a 9.7 clip per game.

And Eckman did take credit for at least one major coaching move. "I made one big change and that won me a pennant," he said. "I took George Yardley and made him a starter. He and Paul Birch (the former Pistons coach) didn't get along. But I had watched Yardley play in an exhibition game, and he could jump out of the building. And he could shoot. I had to have something that

George Yardley rebounds in 1956 while Corky Devlin looks upcourt.

but with 30 seconds left, the Pistons had cut it to 85-84. With seven seconds left on the game clock and time running down on the shot clock, Rocha hit a 25-foot set shot for the final margin.

From there, the series turned to Zollner's heartbreak. The owner of a piston factory, Zollner had nurtured basketball in the northern Indiana city since 1941. For years, the team had played its games in Fort Wayne's North Side High School, until Zollner had finally convinced the city to build an arena. But few people had figured the Pistons would be good enough to make it to the Finals. So the arena was scheduled for another event, a bowling tournament, that spring of 1955. Zollner was bitterly frustrated that the Finals had to be played in Indianapolis, where his team had only a marginal following. "He was really disappointed," Syracuse owner Danny Biasone said of Zollner. "He said, 'I'm moving the team to Detroit.' And that's what he eventually did."

Only 3,200 fans showed up April 3 to see the Pistons win, 96-89, in Indianapolis. Mel Hutchins rebounded like a madman and scored 22, as Fort Wayne opened as much as a 15-point lead in the second half. Rocha and Schayes scored 21 each for Syracuse, but the Pistons countered with balance.

Fort Wayne then evened the series at 2-2 in Game Four, also in Indianapolis, 109-102, despite 28 points by Schayes. The Nats were troubled by poor shooting, hitting just 32 of 103 shots from the field. At one point the Pistons led, 80-62.

In Game Five, the Pistons took a 3-2 lead with a hairy 74-71 win. They had run up a 15-point lead, only to see the Nats pull close again in the second half. Then in the third period, the action took a bizarre turn.

"We were playing them," the Nats' Paul Seymour said. "All of a sudden there was an explosion. We jumped a mile. We thought a bomb went off. A guy behind the bench had gotten pissed off and thrown a chair. We turned around and it was this little bitty guy sitting there sheepishly."

"It went flying over our heads on the bench and went out on the floor," recalled Syracuse guard (and future Purdue athletic director) George King.

King said something curt to the guy who had thrown the chair, and the man was led away by police. The action resumed, and the Nats cut the lead to 72-71 with just over a minute remaining. Rocha, however, missed a key shot, and the Pistons' Frank Brian hit two free throws at the end for the final margin.

Immediately fans crowded the floor and seemed intent on preventing the Nats from leaving. One guy in particular blocked their way until Syracuse coach Al Cervi took charge,

---

Although the Pistons led 3-2 in the series, the Nats had reason for confidence. The final two games would be played in the Syracuse War Memorial, where the Pistons hadn't won in six seasons.

George King recalled.

"Cervi grabbed the guy by the front of the shirt and ripped it right off him," King said.

"I grabbed the guy by the neck," Cervi said. "When I yanked, his tie came away in my hand. 'Get out of my way,' I said. They opened up and I went through."

A short time later, King learned he had been charged with making threatening statements in connection with the chair-throwing incident. It seemed that the man who threw the chair was an off-duty policeman who obtained a warrant against King. The matter was settled when authorities said King could merely apologize for his language. King didn't think he had anything to apologize for, but team officials told him to do so just to get the matter behind them. King reluctantly agreed.

Although the Pistons led 3-2 in the series, the Nats had reason for confidence. The final two games would be played in the Syracuse War

Memorial, where the Pistons hadn't won in six seasons. They didn't play scared, though. Fort Wayne took an immediate lead and extended it to as much as 10 points in the first half.

The brouhaha atmosphere continued to haunt the series. In the second period, the Nats' Wally Osterkorn and the Pistons' Don Meineke traded punches, an outbreak that brought the fans onto the War Memorial floor. After a time, police restored order and the game continued.

Shooting his jumper, Yardley fired the Pistons (he would finish the game with 31) and lifted them to a 74-68 lead at the end of the third. The Nats finally took the lead with just over four minutes left when Earl Lloyd hit a set shot. At the 90-second mark, the Pistons tied it at 103. But then the Nats' rookie center, Johnny "Red" Kerr hit a jump shot, and Dick Farley tipped in a miss to give Syracuse the lead. After hitting their free throws, the Nats evened the series at three all with a 109-104 win. Even the NBA's newly installed shot clock hadn't saved it from being a foulfest. Syracuse had been whistled for 31 transgressions, Fort Wayne for 33.

Game Seven was just as intense. The Pistons ran up a big lead, as many as 17 at one point in the second period. But Syracuse closed to 53-47 by the half and pulled tight down the stretch. Schayes hit two free throws with 80 seconds left to give the Nats a 91-90 lead, but Yardley tied it moments later with a free throw. Then with 12 seconds left, King, a 61-percent free throw shooter, was fouled and went to the line for two. He missed the first and hit the second, giving Syracuse a 92-91 lead. The Pistons' Frankie Brian inbounded the ball to Andy Phillip, who attempted to go left on Paul Seymour. Seymour nudged him enough to set up King for a steal. There was no call, and like that, the Nats had their first title.

"I bumped the crap out of Andy," Seymour admitted. "For years after that, whenever he'd see me, he'd tell me, 'You got away with the big foul.' I bumped him a little, King was there,

Piston Larry Foust, Paul Seymour of the Syracuse Nationals, Piston Andy Phillip (a Hall of Famer), and Dolph Schayes of Syracuse pose at the 1955 All-Star game.

and that was it."

Some thought it poetic justice, that Eckman, the former official, had been done in by the zebras.

"It was there," Eckman said of the foul. "Lou Eisenstein (the official) choked up and lost his guts. Earlier in the game, when we were ahead by 17, he called a technical on Frankie Brian that got them going."

As for Danny Biasone, he was elated. "It was a tough game to lose," he said. "I would have felt bad myself."

Mostly, though, he was glad of the clock's role. Biasone had fought for years to have a shot clock installed for NBA games. When it was added in 1954, Biasone had been ready with a quick team to take advantage of the change.

"If it wasn't for the shot clock, it would have been the dullest game in history," he said of Game Seven. "Fort Wayne was up by 17. Under the old rules, they'd have gone into a stall. Then there'd have been a flurry of fouls."

Instead of a boring the game, the few thousand fans who saw it were treated to a hugely entertaining finals. All considered, though, the Pistons would rather have had the rings.

1956

The Syracuse Nationals weren't the first team to self-destruct after a championship season, and they certainly wouldn't be the last. They had some conflicts going throughout the 1955-56 season, evidenced by their last-place finish in the Eastern Division.

Their 35-37 record, however, was good enough to get them into the

playoffs, where they knocked off Boston in the first round, only to lose to Philadelphia in the Eastern finals, 3-2. When it was all over, the players voted unanimously to cut Cervi out of a share of playoff money.

"It wasn't good," Dolph Schayes said. "The players resented a lot of things Cervi did."

Charlie Eckman, meanwhile, avoided such troubles by having a clause in his contract stating that his playoff bonus wouldn't be taken as a cut from the players' shares.

That was one of the keys to his success. Plus the fact that he picked his spots. "Never once," he said, "did I give them any hell or talk to them about a loss. You can't talk to a ball player after a game. They're too tired to listen."

Even so, the Pistons had their problems. Most of them stemmed

Dick Farley of Syracuse beats the Pistons with a last-minute tap-in in Game Six of the 1955 Finals.

back to an incident that occured the season before Eckman's arrival. Jack Molinas, a talented Pistons rookie, had been deeply involved in gambling and was forced out of the league (he would later become a major figure in the college point-shaving scandals of 1961). Fred Zollner was a deeply suspicious man, and the incident made him more so. Although there was no evidence to suggest any of his other players were doing business with gamblers, he seemed certain that was the case.

Zollner hired a former Fort Wayne police detective to shadow the team throughout the 1955-56 season, Eckman said. "Zollner had a private eye. All year he arrived ahead of us in most towns."

Despite the distractions and the pressure on certain players that Zollner believed to be doing business, the Pistons made it back to the Finals. They got there by winning the weak Western Division with a 37-35 record, then nosing St. Louis in the divisional finals, 3-2.

Now in his third year, Yardley had developed into a star. "He could get rid of the ball as quick as anybody," Eckman said. "He wasn't big, but he could give that head fake. Bingo. The shot was up and gone."

The Pistons' talent, though, could carry them only so far. Like the Nats, Fort Wayne seemed to be shouldering too many troubles to win a championship. That honor would fall to a team, the Philadelphia Warriors, that had found an answer to its own troubles.

The Warriors had always seemed to have plenty of talent. First there was lantern-jawed center Neil Johnston, a 6'8" veteran out of Ohio State. His hook shot made him what you might call a mid '50s version of a scoring machine. For three straight seasons, 1952-55, he had led the league in scoring. To go with him, the Warriors had 6'4" Paul Arizin, the jump-shooting forward who had led the league in scoring in 1951 and finished number two behind teammate Johnston in '55.

But with the top two scorers in the league, the Warriors had finished

dead last in the Eastern in '55. It was obvious they needed something more. They got it in the draft that spring in the form of 6'6" Thomas Joseph Gola, the son of a Philadelphia policeman. Gola had played his college ball right in Philly at LaSalle. As a freshman, Gola had helped his team to the NIT championship and won a share of the MVP award for himself. Two seasons later, he carried LaSalle to the NCAA championship and was named the Final Four's Most Outstanding Player.

"I have never seen one player control a game by himself as well as Gola does," LaSalle coach Ken

Zollner hired a former Fort Wayne Police detective to shadow the team throughout the 1955-56 season, Eckman said.

Loeffler told reporters.

He had brought LaSalle instant success, and the Warriors figured he would do the same for them. They figured right.

"They won it because they got Gola," Charlie Eckman said.

With Gola in the backcourt, the Warriors were clearly the best team in the league in 1955-56. They finished with the best record, 45-27, six games ahead of Red Auerbach's Celtics.

They fought off Syracuse in the Eastern finals, which left them tired and tentative in Game One of the league Finals. The series opened in Philadelphia, before a crowd of 4,100. What they say was ugly but effective. The best defensive team in the league, the Pistons, shut down the Philly offense in the second period, allowing just one field goal in nearly nine minutes. Midway through the period, the Pistons took a 37-22 lead.

But in the third period, the Warriors turned a nine-point deficit into a nine-point lead, 73-64. The Pistons' frontcourt—Hutchins, Foust and Bob

Houbregs—had held Johnston, the high-scoring Philly center, to three field goals (one in the first half). But Ernie Beck, Gola and Arizin carried the Warriors.

The Pistons fought back in the fourth but never got close than four, the final margin at 98-94. Arizin had scored 28 for the Warriors, and Yardley matched that with 27 for the Pistons..

Game Two was played in Fort Wayne, where the Pistons evened the series at one-all with an 84-83 win. The big points came on free throws from Yardley with 43 seconds left.

The Warriors had a chance to win it, but Yardley blocked Arizin's shot underneath to preserve the victory.

Arizin had again scored big, finishing with 27 points. "Arizin was asthmatic," Eckman said. "He was always clearing his nose. Everybody was scared to get close to him. They thought he had germs. I told them it was asthma, not germs. Yardley said Arizin was spittin' and slingin' snot on him. I told Yardley to spit back on him."

The close series brought the city of Philadelphia to life, and a record crowd of 11,698 packed Convention Hall for Game Three. Arizin again wheezed his way to 27 points, and Johnston finally found his hook shot and added 20. Even so, the Pistons led 51-48 at the half. The Warriors, however, surged in the second half and took a 2-1 lead with a 100-96 win. Foust led the Pistons with 19.

Game Four was scheduled for April 5 in Fort Wayne, where Philadelphia hadn't won in four years. Although they had the series lead, the Warriors were clearly troubled. Senesky remembered that during a layover in Pittsburgh while traveling to Fort Wayne, Gola told his teammates, "Don't worry. We're gonna get the money."

"It was tough to win on the road back then," Senesky said. "But you had confidence in Tommy. You could rely on him. He wasn't gonna throw the ball away. You could just about always get a good shot out of him. He knew the game. He was a smart player."

They played smartly as a team in

Game Four. None was smarter than Arizin, who was unstoppable for the fourth straight came. He hit just about everything he put up. Reverse layups. Corner jump shots. Long sets. Short hooks. And he was eight for eight from the line to finish with 30 points. George added 20, Gola 19 and Johnston 18, to give Philly its first victory in Fort Wayne since February 1952.

The Warriors took a 106-100 lead with just under two minutes left. But Foust and Yardley hit field goals and Hutchins made a free throw to pull the Pistons to 106-105 with 40 seconds to go. Then George Dempsey made a free throw to move Philadelphia ahead, 107-105. As time expired, Corky Devlin of the Pistons threw up a long prayer that went in. But the officials ruled it was after the buzzer.

Ahead 3-1, the Warriors headed home confident that they could close it out. Once there, they turned on the offense. Arizin scored 26 and Graboski 29. Yardley put in 30 for the Pistons, but it wasn't enough. Philly stayed strong down the stetch to take the title, 98-88.

IN AND OUT AT DETROIT

Fred Zollner remembered his disappointment from the 1955 Finals and moved the Pistons to Detroit for the 1957-58 season. Charlie Eckman went along as coach.

But Zollner remained suspicious that some players were doing business with gamblers, so he broke up the team, trading away key parts. That spelled the end for the ref who would be coach.

"It wasn't a good situation," Eckman said of the team's first year in Motown. "We had no place to practice, and nobody cared."

Worst of all, the season opened against the defending champion Boston Celtics with Bill Russell. Before Russell had arrived in the fall of 1956, Boston coach Red Auerbach had struggled like the other coaches in the league. But Russell was a dominant player, who would lead Boston to 11 titles in 13 seasons.

Eckman recalled that the season

Dick Farley of Syracuse would later become a Piston.

before Russell arrived, Boston was playing the Pistons late in the season. Eckman's team had secured first place in the Western, while Auerbach's was battling to make the Eastern playoffs.

"Red walked by me before the game," Eckman recalled, "and said, 'Take it easy on me. I got to get to the playoffs.' I told him, 'I'm gonna play everybody 12 minutes in this ball game. If you can't beat me tonight, you can't beat me.'"

The Celtics won, and a few years later Eckman thought Auerbach would acknowledge the debt. On opening night in Detroit, he walked up to Auerbach before the game and asked him to take it easy on a bad team, Eckman recalled. "That S.O.B. beat us by 51 points on opening night. He's all heart. He had no business running it up on us like that."

The humiliating loss at home left Zollner thinking it might be time for a change. A couple of weeks into the season, the Pistons stood at 9-16, when Zollner met with his coach. Eckman remembers the exchange something like this:

Zollner: "Well, how'd you do last

night?"

Eckman: "We got beat by 14."

Zollner: "What's the matter with the team?"

Eckman: "It's a horseshit team."

Zollner: "I think we're gonna have to make a change in your department."

"It took me a minute," Eckman recalled, "to realize I was a one-man department."

Getting fired in Detroit didn't spell the end for Eckman. Zollner allowed him to resign and paid him a nice settlement.

Eckman went on to become a first-rate college official, working for years in the Atlantic Coast Conference. He became the only official to referee the NBA Finals, the NCAA tournament Finals, the National Invitational Tournament Finals and to coach in the NBA Finals and the NBA All-Star Game.

To many, that would seem like quite an accomplishment. But to Eckman, it was easy. At least the coaching was, he said. "It's not hard to coach. You match personnel, and you keep fresh ballplayers in there. It's a simple game."

Piston Flashbacks

The Pistons' Gene Shue (white shirt) battles the Lakers' Elgin Baylor (22) during the 1962 Western Division championship series. Jerry West (44) and Frank Selvy (11) watch the action. Los Angeles won, 4-2.

Boston's Bob Cousy drives against the Pistons in March 1963. The Pistons are Bob Ferry (16) and Don Ohl (10).

Clifford Ray of the Golden State Warriors jams in 1975 as Bob Lanier (16) and other Pistons look on.

Former Pistons player/coach Dave DeBusschere of New York scores against his old team in 1969.

Piston
Profiles

MARK AGUIRRE

Postion: Forward
Height: 6'6"
Weight: 232
High School: Chicago Westinghouse
College: DePaul '82
Birthdate: 12-10-59
When Drafted: First overall, Dallas 1981 as a hardship
How Acquired: Acquired from the Dallas Mavericks on February 15 in the Nba:s biggest and most controversial trade of the season
Pro Experience: 11 years
Married: Angela
Children: Angelei
Residence: Bloomfield Hills, MI

LAST SEASON: For the second straight season, he spent most of the campaign coming of the bench...Did open the season as the team's starting small forward through the first five games, then moved back to the bench...Started a total of 13 games during 1990-91...Detroit was 7-6 with him in the starting lineup...The Pistons were 42-23 when he came off the bench...Missed a total of four games due to injury...For the second straight season, his scoring average dipped below 15.0 points per game...Has now played two full seasons with the Pistons...

AS A PRO: Acquired from the Dallas Mavericks on February 15, 1989 in the NBA's biggest and most controversial trade of that season...While acquiring Aguirre, the Pistons sent Adrian Dantley and Detroit's 1991 number-one draft choice to the Dallas Mavericks...Including the playoffs, the Pistons were 45-8 with Aguirre, sporting a 44-6 record when he was in the starting lineup during that first year...Since he has been with the Pistons, the team has recorded a 176-76 record with two NBA World Championships...Through 10 NBA seasons, he has already eclipsed better than 16,000 career points...In 1984 was the first-ever Maverick to play in an All-Star Game...Has now played in three mid-season classics...Holds Maverick records for points in a quarter (24), a half (32), points in a game (49) and a season (2,330)...Was the first player selected in the 1981 NBA draft, while fellow Chicagoan and Pistons' team captain Isiah Thomas was the second player selected in that same college draft...

AS A COLLEGIAN: Led Depaul to a 79-10 record in his three years while averaging 24.5 points per game...Two-time consensus All-American...Received several player of the year honors during the post-season of his sophomore and junior seasons...Played in the Final Four as a freshman...Left Depaul after his junior season...Played on the 1980 United States Olympic Team...

PERSONAL: In 1988, married the former Angela Bowman on All-Star Saturday in Chicago, his hometown...Included in his wedding party were Isiah Thomas and Magic Johnson...Was cut the first time he tried out for his grade school team...Avid golfer who plays nearly every day during the off-season...

NBA CAREER RECORD

TEAM-YR	GP	MIN	FGM	FGA	PCT	FTM	FTA	PCT	OFF	DEF	REB	AVE	AST	PF-DQ	ST	BL	PTS	AVE	HI
DAL.'82	51	1468	381	820	.465	168	247	.680	89	160	249	4.9	164	152-0	37	22	955	18.7	42
DAL.'83	81	2784	767	1589	.483	429	589	.728	191	317	508	6.3	332	247-5	80	26	1979	24.4	44
DAL.'84	79	2900	925	1765	.524	465	621	.749	161	308	469	5.9	358	246-5	80	22	2330	29.5	46
DAL.'85	80	2699	794	1569	.506	440	580	.759	188	289	477	6.0	249	250-3	60	24	2055	25.7	49
DAL.'86	74	2501	666	1327	.503	318	451	.705	177	268	445	6.0	339	229-6	62	14	1670	22.6	42
DAL.'87	80	2663	787	1590	.495	429	557	.770	181	246	427	5.3	254	243-4	84	30	2056	25.7	43
DAL.'88	77	2610	746	1571	.475	388	504	.770	182	252	434	5.6	278	223-1	70	57	1932	25.1	38
DL-DT '89	80	2597	586	1270	.461	288	393	.733	146	240	386	4.8	278	229-2	45	36	1511	18.9	41
DET.'90	78	2005	438	898	.487	192	254	.756	117	188	305	3.9	145	201-2	34	19	1099	14.1	31
DET.'91	78	2006	420	909	.462	240	317	.757	134	240	374	4.8	139	209- 2	47	20	1104	14.2	29
TOTALS	758	24233	6510	13308	.489	3357	4513	.743	1566	2508	4074	5.4	2536	2229-30	599	270	16691	22.0	49

NBA HIGHS

51	21	40		14	20		9	10	15		17		5	3	49

3-POINT FIELD GOALS: 1981-82, 25-71 (.352); 1982-83, 16-76 (.211); 1983-84, 15-56 (.268); 1984-85, 27-85 (.318); 1985-86, 16-56 (.286); 1986-87, 53-150 (.353); 1987-88, 52-172 (.302); 1988-89, 51-174 (.293), 1989-90, 31-93 (.333), 1990-91, 24-78 (.308).
CAREER: 310-1011 (.307).

NBA PLAYOFF RECORD

TEAM-YR	GP	MIN	FGM	FGA	PCT	FTM	FTA	PCT	OFF	DEF	REB	AST	PF-DQ	ST	BL	PTS	AVE
DALL. '84	10	350	88	184	.478	44	57	.772	21	55	76	32	34- 2	5	5	220	22.0
DALL. '85	4	164	44	89	.494	27	32	.844	16	14	30	16	16- 1	3	0	116	29.0
DALL. '86	10	345	105	214	.491	35	55	.636	21	50	71	54	28- 1	9	0	247	24.7
DALL. '87	4	130	31	62	.500	23	30	.767	11	13	24	8	15- 1	8	0	85	21.3
DALL. '88	17	558	147	294	.500	60	86	.698	34	66	100	56	49- 0	14	9	367	21.6
DET. '89	17	462	89	182	.489	28	38	.737	26	49	75	28	38- 0	8	3	274	12.6
DET. '90	20	439	86	184	.467	39	52	.750	31	60	91	27	51- 0	10	3	219	11.0
DET. '91	15	397	90	178	.506	42	51	.824	17	44	61	29	41- 0	12	1	234	15.6
TOTALS	97	2845	680	1387	.490	298	401	.743	177	351	528	250	272-5	69	21	1762	18.2

PLAYOFF HIGHS

19	30		11	13			17	10		39

3-POINT FIELD GOALS: 1983-84, 0-5; 1984-85, 1-2 (.500); 1985-86, 2-6 (.333); 1986-87, 0-4; 1987-88, 13-34 (.382); 1988-89, 8-29 (.276); 1989-90, 8-24 (.333). 1990-91, 12-33 (.364).
CAREER: 43-137 (.310).

NBA ALL-STAR RECORD

TEAM-YR	GP	MIN	FGM	FGA	PCT	FTM	FTA	PCT	OFF	DEF	REB	AST	PF-DQ	ST	BL	PTS	AVE
DALL '84	1	13	5	8	.625	3	4	.750	1	0	1	2	2- 0	1	1	13	13.0
DALL '87	1	17	3	6	.500	2	3	.667	1	1	2	1	1- 0	0	0	9	9.0
DALL '88	1	12	5	10	.500	3	3	1	0	1	1	1	3- O	1	0	14	14.0
TOTALS	3	42	13	24	.542	8	10	.800	2	2	4	4	6- 0	2	1	36	12.0

WILLIAM BEDFORD

Position: Center
Height: 7'1"
Weight: 252
High School: Melrose, Memphis, TN
College: Memphis State '87 (Criminal Justice Major)
Birthdate: 12-14-63
When Drafted: First Round (6th Overall) Phoenix, 1986
How Acquired: From Phoenix for the Pistons' Number-One Draft Pick in 1988
Pro Experience: Four Years
Married: Pamela
Children: Diaundra
Residence: Rochester Hills, MI

LAST SEASON: Played in a career high 60 games with the Pistons...Recorded his career high of 20 points versus Denver on Jan. 2...Started the final four games of the regular season, his first ever starts as a Piston...

AS A PRO: Has been a member of the Pistons' roster for each of the last two seasons...Did not play in any games with the Pistons during the 1988-89 season...Spent most of that year in the Adult Substance Abuse Program in Van Nuys, California...On March 30, 1988, he admitted to a drug dependency problem and has not played in a regular season NBA game since that time...Played in just 38 games during his first season (1987-88) with the Pistons...He admitted to a drug dependency problem on March 30, 1988 and was admitted to the Adult Substance Abuse Program in Van Nuys, California under the direction of Dr. Rex Fine...Acquired by the Pistons on June 21, 1987 from the Phoenix Suns for Detroit's number-one draft pick in the 1988 NBA draft...Had a very slow start with the Suns, then suffered torn knee ligaments and had arthroscopic surgery in October of 1986...Entered the NBA after his junior season...

AS A COLLEGIAN: Named Third Team All-American by the Associated Press and was First Team All-Metro Conference in 1986...Finished second behind Keith Lee with 234 career blocked shots at Memphis State...In 1986, he led the Tigers in scoring (17.3), rebounding (8.5), field-goal percentage (.584) and blocked shots (86)...Enjoyed career highs of 30 points and 18 rebounds versus Middle Tennessee State in 1986...Sports Illustrated rated him the number-one true center in the 1986 NBA College Draft...Memphis State qualified for the NCAA Tournament all three seasons he was there, including one trip to the Final Four...Memphis State was 85-17 during his three-year career...

PERSONAL: Married just prior to the start of the 1987-88 Pistons season to the former Pamela Hicks...Born December 14, 1963 in Memphis, Tennessee...Has three sisters...At Memphis State, he majored in Criminal Justice and was a member of the Phi Beta Sigma Fraternity...

NBA CAREER RECORD

TEAM-YR	GP	MIN	FGM	FGA	PCT	FTM	FTA	PCT	OFF	DEF	REB	AVE	AST	PF-DQ	STE	BLO	PTS	AVE	HI
PHO.'87	50	979	142	358	.397	50	86	.581	79	167	246	4.9	57	125- 1	18	37	334	6.7	17
DET.'08	38	298	44	101	.436	13	23	.565	27	38	65	1.7	4	47- 0	8	17	101	2.7	14
DET.'90	42	246	54	125	.432	9	22	.409	15	43	58	1.4	4	39- 0	3	17	118	2.8	13
DET.'91	60	562	106	242	.438	55	78	.705	55	76	131	2.2	32	76- 0	2	36	272	4.5	20
TOTALS	190	2085	346	826	.419	127	209	.608	176	324	500	2.6	97	287- 1	31	107	825	4.3	20

NBA HIGHS

	34	8	18		9	9		6	8	13		4		3	5	20		

3-POINT FIELD GOALS: 1986-87, 0-1 (.000); 1989-90, 1-6 (.167); 1990-91, 5-13 (.385).   CAREER: 6-20 (.300).

NBA PLAYOFF RECORD

TEAM-YR	GP	MIN	FGM	FGA	PCT	FTM	FTA	PCT	OFF	DEF	REB	AST	PF-DQ	ST	BL	PTS	AVE	
DET. '90	5	19	1	6	.167	2	2	1	0	2	2	0	4- 0	0	1	4	0.8	
DET. '91	8	65	5	24	.208	9	14	.643	9	13	22	2.8	4	14- 0	2	4	19	2.4	
TOTALS	13	84	6	30	.200	11	16	.687	9	15	24	3.2	4	18- 0	2	5	23	1.7	

PLAYOFF HIGHS

	16	3	9		4	4				9	2			2	7	

3-POINT FIELD GOALS: 1990-91, 0-2 (.000).

JOE DUMARS

Position: Guard
Height: 6'3"
Weight: 195
College: McNeese State '85 (Business Management Major)
High School: Natchitoches-Central (LA)
Birthdate: 5/24/63
Birthplace: Natchitoches, LA
When Drafted: First Round (18th Overall) Detroit, 1985
How Acquired: College Draft
Pro Experience: Six Years
Married: Debbie
Residence: Burmingham, MI

LAST SEASON: Appeared in his second straight NBA All-Star Game...Made his first All-Star start, replacing the injured Isiah Thomas...Became the first Piston since 1986-87 to log more than 3,000 minutes...Each year in the NBA his scoring average has increased and 1990-91 was the same story...Finished by averaging a career-best 20.4 points per game marking the sixth straight season he's increased his scoring output...Was the Pistons' leading scorer for the first time in his career...Set the all-time Pistons' record by connecting on 62 straight free throws, the fourth longest streak in NBA history...Eclipsed John Long's club-record 51 straight made free throws...Twice tied his career-high by finishing with 42 points...Selected to the NBA's Second Team All-Defense, after being selected to the first team in each of the previous two seasons...

AS A PRO: No longer considered one of the league's most underrated guards after two straight All-Star Game selections...Named the **Most Valuable Player** in the 1989 NBA

Finals, leading the Pistons to the first of two NBA Championships...In the 1989 Finals he led Detroit with a 27.3 points per game average in the four-game sweep of the Lakers...Three times he's scored his career high of 42 points...His first 42-point effort came on April 12, 1989...In that game, he tied the all-time club record for points in a quarter with 24 in the third...Also, he scored 17 straight points, the second most consecutive points total scored in Pistons' history...Twice during his career, he's broken his left hand, his only serious injuries since joining the NBA...After being inserted into the team's starting lineup during the middle of his rookie season, he has remained the team's starting off-guard since that time...Named to the NBA All-Rookie First Team in 1985-86...

AS A COLLEGIAN: Four-time All-Southland Conference selection...Southland Conference leading scorer in 1982, 1984 and 1985...Ranked sixth in the nation in scoring in 1984, averaging 26.4 points per game...All-time McNeese State scoring leader...Holds virtually every McNeese State scoring record...Finished his collegiate career with a 22.3 scoring average...Played in the 1984 U.S. Olympic Trials...Second-leading, all-time Southland Conference scoring leader behind Dwight Lamar...Still ranks among the nation's top 20 all-time leading scorers...

PERSONAL: Older brother David played pro football in the now defunct United States Football League...Comes from a football-oriented family...Has five brothers and one sister...In the 1984-85 McNeese State Media Guide, he listed his favorite athlete as the Pistons' Isiah Thomas...Married in September of 1989 to the former Debbie Nelson...

NBA CAREER RECORD

TEAM-YR	GP	MIN	FGM	FGA	PCT	FTM	FTA	PCT	OFF	DEF	REB	AVE	AST	PF-DQ	ST	BL	PTS	AVE	HI
DET.'86	82	1957	287	597	.481	190	238	.798	60	59	119	1.4	390	200-1	66	11	769	9.4	22
DET.'87	79	2439	369	749	.493	184	246	.748	50	117	167	2.1	352	194-1	83	5	931	11.8	24
DET.'88	82	2732	453	960	.472	251	308	.815	63	137	200	2.4	387	155-1	87	15	1161	14.1	25
DET.'89	69	2408	456	903	.505	260	306	.849	57	115	172	2.5	390	103- 1	63	5	1186	17.2	42
DET.'90	75	2578	508	1058	.480	297	330	.900	60	152	212	2.8	368	129- 1	63	2	1335	17.8	34
DET.'91	80	3046	622	1292	.481	371	417	.890	62	125	187	2.3	443	135- 0	89	7	1629	20.4	42
TOTALS	467	15160	2695	5559	.484	1553	1845	.841	352	705	1057	2.3	2330	916- 5	451	45	7011	15.0	42

NBA HIGHS

53	19	26		18	19		5	8	10		14		5	2	42	

3-POINT FIELD GOALS: 1985-86, 5-16 (.313); 1986-87, 9-22 (.409); 1987-88, 4-19 (.210); 1988-89, 14-29 (.483); 1989-90, 22-55 (.400); 1990-91, 41-45 (.311). CAREER: 68-186 (.366)

NBA PLAYOFF RECORD

TEAM-YR	GP	MIN	FGM	FGA	PCT	FTM	FTA	PCT	OFF	DEF	REB	AST	PF-DQ	ST	BL	PTS	AVE
DET.'86	4	147	25	41	.610	10	15	.667	6	7	13	25	16-0	4	0	60	15.0
DET.'87	15	473	78	145	.538	32	41	.780	8	11	19	72	126-0	12	1	190	12.7
DET.'88	23	804	113	247	.457	56	63	.889	18	32	50	112	50-1	13	2	284	12.3
DET.'89	17	620	106	233	.455	87	101	.861	11	33	44	96	31-0	12	1	300	17.6
DET.'90	20	754	130	284	.453	99	113	.876	18	26	44	95	37- 0	22	0	364	18.2
DET. '91	15	588	105	245	.429	82	97	.845	21	29	50	62	33- 1	16	1	309	20.6
TOTALS	94	3386	557	1195	.466	366	430	.851	82	138	220	462	193- 2	79	5	1507	16.0

PLAYOFF HIGHS

15	23		13	17			7	11		35	

3-POINT FIELD GOALS: 1986-87, 2-3 (.667); 1987-88, 2-6 (.333); 1988-89, 1-12 (.083); 1989-90, 5-19 (.263);990-91, 17-42 (.400). CAREER: 27-82 (.330).

NBA ALL-STAR RECORD

TEAM-YR	GP	MIN	FGM	FGA	PCT	FTM	FTA	PCT	OFF	DEF	REB	AST	PF-DQ	ST	BL	PTS	AVE
DET. '90	1	18	3	4	.750	1	2	.500	0	1	1	5	0- 0	0	0	9	9
DET. '91	1	15	1	4	.250	0	0	.000	1	1	2	1	1- 0	0	0	2	2.0
TOTALS	2	33	4	8	.500	1	2	.500	1	2	3	6	1- 0	0	0	11	5.5

3-POINT FIELD GOALS: 1990-91, 0-1 (.000).

BILL LAIMBEER

Position: Center
Height: 6'11"
Weight: 245
College: Notre Dame (Degree in Economics)
High School: Palos Verdes, CA
Birthdate: 5/19/57
Birthplace: Boston, MA
When Drafted: Third Round (65th Overall) Cleveland, 1979
How Acquired: From Cleveland with Kenny Carr for Phil Hubbard, Paul Mokeski, 1982 First Round Draft Choice, 1982 Second Round Draft Choice
Pro Experience: 11 Years
Nickname: Lambs
Married: Chris (1979)
Children: Eric William and Keriann
Residence: Orchard Lake, MI

LAST SEASON: Became the Pistons' all-time career rebounding leader surpassing Bob Lanier's total of 8,063 during the 1990-91 season...Entering the 1991-92 season, he's hauled down 8,504 rebounds as a Piston...For the second straight season, he did not lead the team in rebounding...Was the Pistons' leading rebounder for seven straight seasons, before losing the team title to Dennis Rodman in each of the last two seasons...For the sixth straight season, he connected on better than 80 percent from the free-throw line...

AS A PRO: Needs just 526 rebounds and he will reach the 10,000 career rebound total, entering the season with 9,474 career rebounds...In his career, he's missed just three games, two due to suspension and one due to a Coach's Decision while a member of the Cleveland Cavaliers...Shares the NBA Finals record with six three-pointers made against Portland in Game Two of the 1990 NBA Finals...Has the fourth longest consecutive games played streak with 685, although it was snapped due to fighting suspension...Twice he's grabbed 9 defensive rebounds in a quarter, an all-time Pistons' record...Has now averaged better than double figures in points for nine straight seasons...Went over the 10,000 career point total during the season 1988-89 season...Ranks in the top 10 of seven Pistons' all-time statistical categories...Came to the Pistons from Cleveland along with Kenny Carr in a deal that was made 9 minutes prior to the NBA trading deadline on Feb. 16, 1982...Started his first game with the Pistons and every one since...Spent the 1979-80 in Italy (22 points per game) after being drafted by Cleveland in the third round of the 1979 NBA draft...Has been named to the NBA All-Star Team four times...Won the NBA rebounding title in 1985-86 when he averaged a career best 13.1 rebounds per game...

AS A COLLEGIAN: College teammate of former Piston Kelly Tripucka when the two were at Notre Dame...Made one appearance in the Final Four...As a senior at Notre Dame, his team was eliminated by eventual NCAA Champion Michigan State...

PERSONAL: High School All-American and two-time All-State pick in California...Played baseball and football in high school...In golf, has a one handicap and finished second in the 1991 Celebrity Golf Classic in Lake Tahoe last July...Has organized the Bill Laimbeer 7-Eleven Muscular Dystrophy Golf Tournament each of the last seven summers...During that time, he's raised over $300,000 for MDA...Would love to play tournament golf when his playing days are complete...He and his wife Chris are the parents of two children Eric and Keriann...

NBA CAREER RECORD

TEAM-YR	GP	MIN	FGM	FGA	PCT	FTM	FTA	PCT	OFF	DEF	REB	AVE	AST	PF-DQ	ST	BLO	PTS	AVE	HI
CLE.'81	81	2460	337	670	.503	117	153	.765	266	427	693	8.6	216	332-1	456	78	791	9.8	26
CL-D'82	80	1829	265	36	.494	184	232	.793	234	383	617	7.7	100	296-5	39	64	718	9.0	30
DET.'83	82	2871	436	877	.497	245	310	.790	282	711	993	12.1	263	320-9	51	118	1119	13.6	30
DET.'84	82	2864	553	1044	.530	316	365	.866	329	674	1003	12.2	149	273-4	49	84	1422	17.3	33
DET.'85	82	2892	595	1177	.506	244	306	.797	295	718	1013	12.4	154	308-4	69	71	1438	17.5	35
DET.'86	82	2891	545	1107	.492	266	319	.834	305	770	1075	13.1	146	291-4	59	65	1360	16.6	29
DET.'87	82	2854	506	1010	.501	245	274	.894	243	712	955	11.6	151	283-4	72	69	1263	15.4	30
DET.'88	82	2897	455	923	.493	187	214	.874	165	667	832	10.1	199	284-6	66	78	1110	13.5	30
DET.'89	81	2640	449	900	.499	178	212	.840	138	638	776	9.6	177	259-2	51	100	1106	13.6	32
DET.'90	81	2675	380	785	.484	164	192	.854	166	614	780	9.6	171	278- 4	57	84	981	12.1	31
DET.'91	82	2668	372	778	.478	123	147	.837	173	564	737	9.0	157	242- 3	38	56	904	11.0	25
TOTALS	897	29541	4893	9807	.499	2269	2724	.833	2596	6878	9474	10.6	1883	3167-59	607	867	12212	13.6	35

NBA HIGHS

		51	16	27		12	13		12	20	24		11		5	6	35		

3-POINT FIELD GOALS: 1980-81, 0-0 (.000); 1981-82, 4-13 (.308); 1982-83, 2-13 (.154); 1983-84, 0-11 (.000); 1984-85, 4-18 (.222); 1985-86, 4-14 (.286); 1986-87, 6-21 (.286); 1987-88, 13-39 (.333), 1988-89, 30-86 (.349); 1989-90, 57-158 (.361); 1990-91, 37-125 (.125). CAREER: 155-498 (.311).

NBA PLAYOFF RECORD

TEAM-YR	GP	MIN	FGM	FGA	PCT	FTM	FTA	PCT	OFF	DEF	REB	AST	PF-DQ	ST	BL	PTS	AVE
DET.'84	5	165	29	51	.569	18	20	.900	14	48	62	12	23-2	4	3	76	15.2
DET.'85	9	325	48	107	.449	36	51	.706	36	60	96	15	32-1	7	7	132	14.7
DET.'86	4	168	34	68	.500	21	23	.913	20	36	56	1	19-1	2	3	90	22.5
DET.'87	15	543	84	163	.515	15	24	.625	30	126	156	37	53-2	15	12	184	12.3
DET.'88	23	779	114	250	.456	40	45	.889	43	178	221	44	77-2	18	19	273	11.9
DET.'89	17	497	66	142	.465	25	31	.806	26	114	140	31	55-1	6	8	172	10.1
DET.'90	20	667	91	199	.457	25	29	.862	41	170	211	28	77- 3	23	18	222	11.1
DET. '91	15	446	66	148	.446	27	31	.871	42	80	122	19	54- 0	5	12	164	10.9
TOTALS	93	3144	466	980	.476	180	223	.807	210	732	942	168	336-12	75	70	1149	12.4

PLAYOFF HIGHS

		10	23		13	13			19		6			31	

3-POINT FIELD GOALS: 1984-85, 0-2 (.000); 1985-86, 1-1 (1.000); 1986-87, 1-5 (.200); 1987-88, 5-17 (.294); 1988-89, 15-42 (.357); 1989-90, 15-43 (.349); 1990-91, 5-17 (.290). CAREER: 52-127 (.410).

NBA ALL-STAR RECORD

TEAM-YR	GP	MINS	AVE	FGM	FGA	PCT	FTM	FTA	PCT	OFF	DEF	REB	AVE	AST	PF-DQ	ST	BL	PTS	AVE
DET.'83	1	6	6.0	1	1	1.000	0	0	—	1	0	1	1.0	0	1-0	0	0	2	2.0
DET.'84	1	17	17.0	6	8	.750	1	1	1.000	1	4	5	5.0	0	3-0	1	2	13	13.0
DET.'85	1	11	11.0	2	4	.500	1	2	.500	1	2	3	3.0	1	1-0	0	0	5	5.0
DET.'87	1	11	11.0	4	7	.571	0	0	—	0	2	2	2.0	1	1-2	1	0	8	8.0
TOTALS	4	45	11.3	13	20	.650	2	3	.667	3	8	11	2.8	2	7-0	2	2	28	7.0

DENNIS RODMAN

Position: Forward
Height: 6'8"
Weight: 210
College: Southeastern Oklahoma State '86
High School: South Oak Cliff HS (TX)
Birthdate: 05/13/61
Birthplace: Dallas, TX
When Drafted: Second Round (27th Overall) Detroit, 1986
How Acquired: College Draft
Pro Experience: Five Years
Nickname: Worm
Marital Status: Single
Residence: Dallas, TX

LAST SEASON: For the second straight season, he was named **MasterLock NBA Defensive Player of the Year**...Also, named to the NBA's All Defense First Team...Finished last season as the NBA's second leading rebounder, averaging 12.5 rebounds per game...Set the Pistons' single-season record with 361 offensive rebounds...Became the first Piston since 1985-86 to haul down 1,000 rebounds...For the fourth straight season, he grabbed better than 300 offensive rebounds...Entering the 1991-92 season, he ranks fourth on the NBA's consecutive games played list with 383 straight appearances...Has played in all 82 games for four straight seasons...Won the team rebounding title each of the last two seasons, ending Laimbeer's reign at seven straight...Scored his career high of 34 points versus Denver on Jan. 2, 1991...Grabbed his career high of 24 rebounds versus Indiana on Feb. 13, 1991...

AS A PRO: Two-time NBA Defensive Player of the Year...Three-time NBA All Defense First Team selection...Played in his first NBA All-Star Game during the 1989-90 season, scoring four points...In 1988-89 finished the season as the league's top field-goal percentage shooter, connecting on .595 of his attempts, shattering the all-time Pistons' record in the process...In 1988-89, finished second in the balloting for both the NBA's Defensive Player of the Year and the Sixth Man Award...Had his best game as a pro in Golden State on February 18, 1989 when he scored 32 points and grabbed 21 rebounds, both career highs at the time...Entered the NBA from little-known Southeast Oklahoma State and made an impact with the Pistons immediately...Nicknamed Worm, he suddenly became a Pistons fan favorite during his first year with the club...Has used Northwood Institute Coach Pat Miller as a shooting instructor...

AS A COLLEGIAN: First Team NAIA All-American for three consecutive seasons...Did not play high school basketball and stood only 5'11" after his senior year...After graduation from high school, he grew 7 inches...Played one semester at Cooke County Junior College before transferring...Had 24 points and 19 rebounds in his first collegiate game, then followed with 40 points in his second game...As a sophomore, he scored 42 points and grabbed 24 rebounds in the semi-finals of the District Nine playoffs...Scored a career high of 51 points against Bethany Nazarene in the playoffs...

PERSONAL: His two sisters, Debra and Kim were High School All-Americans and led South Oak Cliff to two state titles...Debra, 6'3", went on to Louisiana Tech, played on a national championship team and was a three-time All-American...Kim was an All-American at Stephen F. Austin...Needless to say, his two sisters influenced him tremendously...An outstanding pinball player...Runs very successful summer basketball camps...

NBA CAREER RECORD

TEAM-YR	GP	MIN	FGM	FGA	PCT	FTM	FTA	PCT.	OFF	DEF	REB	AVE	AST	PF-DQ	ST	BL	PTS	AVE	HI
DET.'87	77	1155	213	391	.545	74	126	.587	163	169	332	4.3	56	166-1	38	48	500	6.5	21
DET.'88	82	2147	398	709	.561	152	284	.535	318	397	715	8.7	110	273-5	75	45	953	11.6	30
DET.'89	82	2208	316	531	.595	97	155	.626	327	445	772	9.4	99	292-5	55	76	735	9.0	32
DET.'90	82	2377	288	496	.581	142	217	.654	336	456	792	9.6	72	276-2	52	60	719	8.8	18
DET.'91	82	2747	276	560	.493	111	176	.631	361	665	1026	12.5	85	281-7	65	55	669	8.2	34
TOTALS	405	10634	1491	2687	.554	576	958	.601	1505	2132	3637	9.0	422	1288-19	285	284	3576	8.8	34

NBA HIGHS

		MIN	FGM	FGA		FTM	FTA				REB		AST		ST	BL	PTS		
		48	15	21		9	12		10	13	24		5		4	4	34		

3-POINT FIELD GOALS: 1986-87, 0-1 (.000); 1987-88, 5-17 (.294); 1988-89, 6-26 (.231); 1989-90, 1-9 (.111); 1990-91, 6-30 (.200).
CAREER: 18-83 (.217).

NBA PLAYOFF RECORD

TEAM-YR	GP	MIN	FGM	FGA	PCT	FTM	FTA	PCT	OFF	DEF	REB	AST	PF-DQ	ST	BL	PTS	AVE
DET.'87	15	245	40	74	.541	18	32	.563	32	39	71	3	48-0	6	17	98	6.5
DET.'88	23	474	71	136	.522	22	54	.407	51	85	136	21	87-1	14	14	164	7.1
DET.'89	17	409	37	70	.529	24	35	.686	56	114	170	16	58-0	6	12	198	5.8
DET.'90	19	560	54	95	.568	18	35	.514	55	106	161	17	62-1	9	13	126	6.6
DET.'91	15	495	41	91	.451	10	24	.417	67	110	177	14	55-1	11	10	94	6.3
TOTALS	89	2183	243	466	.521	92	180	.511	261	454	715	71	310-3	46	66	680	7.6

PLAYOFF HIGHS

			FGM	FGA		FTM	FTA				REB	AST				PTS	
			10	16		6	10				20	3				23	

3-POINT FIELD GOALS: 1987-88, 0-2 (.000); 1988-89, 0-4 (.000); 1989-90, 0-0 (.000); 1990-91, 2-9 (.220).

NBA ALL-STAR RECORD

TEAM-YR	GP	MIN	FGM	FGA	PCT.	FTM	FTA	PCT.	OFF	DEF	REB	AST	PF-DQ	ST	BL	PTS	AVE
DET. '90	1	11	2	4	.500	0	0	0	3	1	4	1	1-0	0	1	4	4

JOHN SALLEY

Position: Forward/Center
Height: 6'11"
Weight: 231
College: Georgia Tech '86 (Degree in Industrial Management)
High School: Canarsie HS, Brooklyn, NY
Birthdate: 05/16/64
Birthplace: Brooklyn, NY
When Drafted: First Round (11th Overall) Detroit, 1986
How Acquired: College Draft
Pro Experience: Five Years
Nickname: Spider
Marital Status: Single
Residence: Brooklyn, NY

LAST SEASON: Completed his fifth season with the Pistons...For the fourth time in five seasons, he blocked 100 shots...Pistons' career playoff leader in blocked shots...Shot a career high 73 percent from the free-throw line during the 1990-91 season...Came off the bench in all but one game...

AS A PRO: Started slowly in his rookie campaign, but has proved to be very consistent since that time...Has already recorded 599 blocked shots in his first five campaigns, which ranks him fourth on the all-time Pistons' blocked shots list...Had

his best game as a pro during his rookie season when he scored 28 points, adding 10 rebounds and 5 blocked shots versus the Milwaukee Bucks on April 5, 1987...Set an all-time Pistons' playoff record with 10 offensive rebounds versus the Washington Bullets in the first round of the 1988 playoffs...In his five seasons, the Pistons have made five straight Eastern Conference Finals appearances and three trips to the Finals...

AS A COLLEGIAN: Finished fourth on the all-time Georgia Tech scoring list with 1,587 points (12.7 points per game), third in all-time FG percentage (.587) and is the school's all-time shotblocker (243)...Started 27 games as a freshman and averaged 11.5 points and 5.7 rebounds per game...Had a career high of 28 points against Monmouth on 1-17-85...Set a school record in his junior season when he connected on .627 of his field goal attempts...

PERSONAL: One of the most outgoing and personable players on the Piston roster...Makes numerous personal appearances on behalf of the club and various charities throughout the year...Entered Georgia Tech as a 6-9, 185-pound forward and continued to add both size and strength...His nickname is Spider because of his long arms...Strengths are quickness, passing and shotblocking...Received his degree from Georgia Tech in the August of 1988...Runs a summer basketball camp...Aspiring comedian who makes appearances and comedy clubs during the year...His personal friends include Eddie Murphy and Spike Lee...

NBA CAREER RECORD

TEAM-YR	GP	MIN	FGM	FGA	PCT	FTM	FTA	PCT	OFF	DEF	REB	AVE	AST	PF-DQ	ST	BL	PTS	AVE	HI
DET.'87	82	1463	163	290	.562	105	171	.614	108	188	296	3.6	54	256- 5	44	125	431	5.3	28
DET.'88	82	2003	258	456	.566	185	261	.709	166	241	402	4.9	113	294- 4	53	137	701	8.5	19
DET.'89	67	1458	166	333	.498	135	195	.692	134	201	335	5	75	197- 3	40	72	467	7	19
DET.'90	82	1914	209	408	.512	174	244	.713	154	285	439	5.3	67	282- 7	51	153	593	7.2	21
DET.'91	74	1649	179	377	.475	186	256	.727	137	190	327	4.4	70	240- 7	52	112	544	7.4	24
TOTALS	387	8487	975	1864	.523	785	1127	.697	699	1105	1799	4.6	379	1269-26	240	599	2736	7.1	28

NBA HIGHS

	40		10	15		11	12		8	8	13		5		3	8	28		

3-POINT FIELD GOALS: 1986-87, 0-1 (.000); 1988-89, 0-2 (.000); 1989-90, 1-4 (.350); 1990-91, 0-1 (.000). CAREER: 1-8 (.125); 1989, 0-2 (.000). CAREER: 0-3 (.000). 0-2 (.000). CAREER: 0-3 (.000).0); 1989-90 , 1-4 (.350).CAREER: 1-7 (.143)

NBA PLAYOFF RECORD

TEAM-YR	GP	MINS	FGM	FGA	PCT	FTM	FTA	PCT	OFF	DEF	REB	AST	PF-DQ	ST	BL	PTS	AVE
DET.'87	15	311	33	66	.500	27	42	.643	30	42	72	11	60-1	3	17	93	6.2
DET.'88	23	623	56	104	.538	49	69	.710	64	91	155	21	88-2	15	37	161	7.0
DET.'89	17	392	58	99	.586	36	54	.667	34	45	79	9	56-0	9	25	152	8.9
DET.'90	20	547	58	122	.475	74	98	.755	57	60	117	20	76- 0	9	33	190	9.5
DET.'91	15	308	38	70	.543	36	60	.600	20	42	62	11	58- 1	6	20	112	7.5
TOTALS	90	2181	243	461	.527	222	323	.687	205	280	485	72	340- 4	42	132	708	7.8

PLAYOFF HIGHS

	10	16		9	12		13	4	23

3-POINT FIELD GOALS: 1987-88, 0-1 (.000); 1988-89, 0-0 (.000); 1989-90, 0-0 (.000); 1990-91, 0-0 (.000). CAREER: 0-1 (.000).

ISIAH THOMAS

Position: Guard
Height: 6'1"
Weight: 185
College: Indiana University '83 (Criminal Justice Degree)
High School: St. Joseph (Westchester, IL)
Birthdate: 4/30/61
Birthplace: Chicago, IL
When Drafted: First Round (2nd Overall) Detroit, 1981
How Acquired: College Draft
Pro Experience: Nine Years
Married: Lynn
Children: Joshua
Residence: Bloomfield Hills, MI

LAST SEASON: Suffered the worst injury of his 10-year NBA career...Was sidelined for nearly 10 weeks and missed 34 games due to wrist surgery, although he did return a month early...Had three bones fused in his right wrist by Dr. Kirk Watson on Jan. 29, 1991...He missed 32 straight games and the Pistons were 18-14 during his absence...Did miss a total of 34 games in the regular season and the Pistons were 19-15...Also missed two playoff games in 1991 due to injury...In his 10-year NBA career, the Pistons are 26-32 when he does not play...Eclipsed the 15,000 points total during the 1990-91 season...Ranks third on the NBA's all-time career assists list, trailing only Magic Johnson and Oscar Robertson...Selected to his 10th straight All-Star Team, although he did not play in the 1991 classic...His scoring average of 16.2 per game was a career low...

AS A PRO: Needs just 359 points to become the all-time leading scorer in Pistons' history...Entering this season, he's scored 15,130 points...He will then surpass Bob Lanier's total of 15,488 points scored...Most Valuable Player in the 1990 NBA Finals when he averaged 27.6 points, 7.0 assists and 5.2 rebounds...Tied the NBA Finals record connecting on four three-pointers in the third quarter of Game Four versus Portland in 1990...Has been named to the NBA All-Star Team in each of his first 10 seasons in the league, although he was unable to play in the 1991 NBA All-Star Game due to injury...Two-time All-Star Game Most Valuable Player, winning the honor in 1984 and 1986...First was MVP in Denver in 1984 when he scored 21 points and added 15 assists...Then in 1986 in Dallas, he scored 30 points, adding 10 assists and 5 steals to gain the honor...All-time Pistons' leader in steals and assists, ranks

third on the all-time Pistons' scoring list entering this season...Set an NBA record for assists in a single season (since broken by John Stockton) when he recorded 1,123 assists in 1984-85 for an average of 13.1 per game...Owns the Pistons' record for consecutive field goals made with 13...Holds the club record for points scored in a quarter with 24...Has had some memorable playoff performances...Scored 25 points in the 3rd quarter of Game 6 versus the Lakers in the 1988 NBA Finals, setting a record for points in a quarter in a Finals' game...Had 24 points in the 3rd quarter versus the Atlanta Hawks in the 1987 playoffs...In the 1990 NBA Finals, he scored 22 points in the third quarter...In Game One of the 1990 NBA Finals he scored 16 points in the fourth quarter (finishing with 33) rallying Detroit from 10 points down with seven minutes remaining...But, maybe his most memorable playoff performance was in the 1984 playoffs versus the New York Knicks when he scored 16 points in 94 seconds in the fourth quarter of the decisive Game 5 of that series...Was drafted by the Pistons second overall in the 1981 NBA College Draft after leaving Indiana after his sophomore season...

AS A COLLEGIAN: Helped lead the Indiana Hoosiers to a 47-17 mark and an NCAA Championship (1981) with two Big Ten titles in his two seasons there...Missed only one game during his collegiate career and started all 63 games he played...All Big Ten as a sophomore...Was a consensus All-American after his sophomore season at Indiana...Top college scoring effort was 39 points versus the University of Michigan...Won 1981 NCAA Tournament Most Outstanding Player Award with 91 points in five games (18.2 points per game)...Member of the 1979 Pan-American Games Gold Medal Team, scoring 21 points in the title game, while leading the team in assists...Starter on the 1981 USA Olympic Team which had a 5-1 record against NBA All-Star Teams...

PERSONAL: Prior to training camp in October of 1988, he signed a contract which will keep him in Detroit for the remainder of his basketball playing career...Youngest of nine children...One of the league's most vocal players in the fight against drug abuse, has made a 12-minute film entitled "Just Say No"...Married in July of 1985 to the former Lynn Kendall...Received his degree in Criminal Justice in August of 1987...Has numerous endorsements which include Toyota and Coca Cola...Isiah's Summer Classic All-Star Game in August of 1990 was played for the benefit of Comic Relief, benefitting the homeless...Authored the book **Bad Boys, An Inside Look at the Detroit Pistons 1988-89 Championship Season**, co-authored by Pistons PR Director Matt Dobek...President of the NBA's Player Association...

NBA CAREER RECORD

TEAM-YR	GP	MIN	FGM	FGA	PCT	FTM	FTA	PCT	OFF	DEF	REB	AVE	AST	PF-DQ	ST	BLO	PTS	AVE	HI
DET.'82	72	2433	453	1068	.424	302	429	.704	57	152	209	2.9	565	253-2	150	17	1225	17.0	34
DET.'83	81	3093	725	1537	.472	368	518	.710	105	223	328	4.0	634	318-8	199	29	1854	22.9	46
DET.'84	82	3007	669	1448	.462	388	529	.733	103	224	327	4.0	914	324-8	204	33	1748	21.3	47
DET.'85	81	3089	646	1410	.458	399	493	.809	114	247	361	4.5	1123	288-8	187	25	1720	21.2	38
DET.'86	77	2790	609	1248	.488	365	462	.790	83	194	277	3.6	830	245-9	171	20	1609	20.9	39
DET.'87	81	3013	626	1353	.463	400	521	.768	82	237	319	3.9	813	251-5	153	20	1671	20.6	36
DET.'88	81	2927	621	1341	.463	305	394	.774	64	214	278	3.4	678	217-0	141	17	1577	19.5	42
DET.'89	80	2924	569	1227	.464	287	351	.818	49	224	273	3.4	663	209-0	133	20	1458	18.2	37
DET.'90	81	2993	579	1322	.438	292	377	.774	74	234	308	3.8	765	206-0	139	19	1492	18.4	37
DET.'91	48	1657	289	665	.435	179	229	.782	35	125	160	3.3	446	118-4	75	10	776	16.2	32
TOTALS	764	27926	5786	12619	.459	3285	4303	.763	766	2074	2840	3.7	7431	2419-44	1552	210	15130	19.8	47

NBA HIGHS

		52	19	34		16	20		6	11	12		25		7	4	47		

3-POINT FIELD GOALS: 1981-82, 17-59 (.288); 1982-83, 36-125 (.288); 1983-84, 22-65 (.338); 1984-85, 29-113 (.257); 1986-87, 19-98 (.194); 1987-88, 30-97 (.309); 1988-89, 33-121 (.273); 1989-90, 42-136 (.309); 1990-91, 19-65 (.292).
CAREER: 275-963 (.286).

NBA PLAYOFF RECORD

TEAM-YR	GP	MIN	FGM	FGA	PCT	FTM	FTA	PCT	OFF	DEF	REB	AST	PF-DQ	ST	BL	PTS	AVE
DET.'84	5	198	39	83	.470	27	35	.771	7	12	19	55	22-1	13	6	107	21.4
DET.'85	9	355	83	166	.500	47	62	.758	11	36	47	101	39-2	19	4	219	24.3
DET.'86	4	163	41	91	.451	24	36	.667	8	14	22	48	17-0	9	3	106	26.5
DET.'87	15	562	134	297	.451	83	110	.755	21	46	67	130	51-1	39	4	361	24.1
DET.'88	23	911	183	419	.437	125	151	.828	26	81	107	201	71-2	66	8	504	21.9
DET.'89	17	633	115	279	.412	71	96	.740	24	49	73	141	39-0	27	4	309	18.2
DET.'90	20	758	148	320	.463	81	102	.794	21	88	109	163	65-1	43	7	409	20.5
DET. '91	13	436	60	149	.403	50	69	.725	13	41	54	111	41-1	13	2	176	13.5
TOTALS	106	4016	803	1804	.445	508	661	.769	131	367	498	950	345-8	229	38	2191	20.1

PLAYOFF HIGHS

TEAM-YR	GP	MIN	FGM	FGA	PCT	FTM	FTA	PCT	OFF	DEF	REB	AST	PF-DQ	ST	BL	PTS	AVE
			18	33		13	17					12	16			43	

3-POINT FIELD GOALS: 1983-84, 2-6 (.333); 1984-85, 6-15 (.400); 1985-86, 0-5 (.000); 1986-87, 10-33 (.303); 1987-88, 13-44 (.295); 1988-89, 8-30 (.267); 1989-90, 32-68 (.471); 1990-91, 6-22 (.270).
CAREER: 77-223 (.350).

NBA ALL-STAR RECORD

TEAM-YR	GP	MIN	FGM	FGA	PCT	FTM	FTA	PCT	OFF	DEF	REB	AST	PF-DQ	ST	BL	PTS	AVE
DET.'82	1	17	5	7	.714	2	4	.500	1	0	1	4	1-0	3	0	12	12.0
DET.'83	1	29	9	14	.643	1	1	1.000	3	1	4	7	0-0	4	6	19	19.0
DET.'84	1	39	9	17	.529	3	3	1.000	2	3	5	15	4-0	4	0	21	21.0
DET.'85	1	25	9	14	.643	1	1	1.000	1	1	2	5	2-0	2	0	22	22.0
DET.'86	1	36	11	19	.579	8	9	.889	0	1	1	10	2-0	5	0	30	30.0
DET.'87	1	24	4	6	.667	8	9	.889	2	1	3	9	3-0	0	0	16	16.0
DET.'88	1	28	4	10	.400	0	0	.000	1	1	2	15	1-0	1	0	8	8.0
DET.'89	1	33	7	13	.538	4	6	.667	1	1	2	14	2-0	0	0	19	19.0
DET.'90	1	27	7	12	.583	0	0	.000	1	3	4	9	0-0	3	0	15	15
DET.'91		DNP - INJURED															
TOTALS	9	258	65	112	.580	27	33	.818	12	12	24	88	15-0	22	0	162	18

3-POINT FIELD GOALS: 1983-84, 0-2 (.000); 1984-85, 3-4 (.750); 1985-86, 0-1 (.000); 1988-89, 1-3 (.333); 1989-90, 1-1 (1.000).
CAREER: 5-11 (.455).

DARRELL WALKER

Position: Guard
Height: 6'4"
Weight: 180
College: University of Arkansas
High School: Corliss (Chicago, IL)
Birthdate: 3/9/61
Birthplace: Chicago, IL
When Drafted: 1983 (12th, 1st round)
How Acquired: Trade
Pro Experience: Eight Years
Married: Felicia
Children: Jarrell and Jarrett
Residence: Little Rock, AK

LAST SEASON: Acquired from the Washington Bullets on Sept. 5,1991 in exchange for two second-round draft choices...Detroit now becomes his fourth NBA stop while he begins his ninth NBA season...Led all NBA guards in rebounding last season with 7.0 caroms per game for the Bullets...Missed a total of 11 games (Bullets were 2-9) due to a strained ligament in his right knee...

AS A PRO: Began his NBA career as a member of the New York Knicks, gaining All-Rookie honors, while setting a then Knicks' record with 127 steals...After three seasons with the Knicks, he was then traded to Denver in October of 1986 for a number-one draft choice...In his only year with the Nuggets, he scored his career high of 39 points versus Utah...Traded to Washington from Denver along with Mark Alarie on Nov. 2, 1987 in exchange for Michael Adams and Jay Vincent...Played four full seasons with the Bullets... Had his best season in the NBA during the 1989-90 campaign when he averaged 9.5 points, 8.8 rebounds and 8.0 assists...

AS A COLLEGIAN: Played three seasons at Arkansas...Transferred to Arkansas from Westart Junior College (Fort Smith, Arkansas)...Was a collegiate teammate at Arkansas with former Piston Scott Hastings...In his senior season at Arkansas, he led the Razorbacks in scoring with 18.2 points per game...

PERSONAL: High School opponent of both Isiah Thomas and Mark Aguirre...Claims his greatest moment as a pro came during the 1984 playoffs while his New York Knicks defeated the Pistons in a grueling five-game series...Once aspired to play professional hockey for the Chicago Black Hawks...Makes his off-season home in Little Rock, Arkansas...

NBA CAREER RECORD

TEAM-YR	GP	MINS	FGM	FGA	PCT.	FTM	FTA	PCT.	OFF	DEF	REBS	AST	PF-DQ	STE	BLO	PTS.	AVE.
N.Y. '84	82	1324	216	518	.417	208	263	.791	74	93	167	284	202- 1	127	15	644	7.9
N.Y. '85	82	2489	430	989	.435	243	347	.700	128	150	278	408	244- 2	167	21	1103	13.5
N.Y. '86	81	2023	324	753	.430	190	277	.686	100	120	220	337	216- 1	146	36	838	10.3
DEN. '87	81	2020	358	742	.482	272	365	.745	157	170	327	282	229- 0	120	37	988	12.2
WASH.'88	52	940	114	291	.392	82	105	.781	43	84	127	100	105- 2	62	10	310	6.0
WASH.'89	79	2565	286	681	.420	142	184	.772	135	372	507	496	215- 2	155	23	714	9.0
WASH.'90	81	2883	316	696	.454	138	201	.687	173	541	714	652	220- 1	139	30	772	9.5
WASH.'91	71	2305	230	535	.430	93	154	.604	140	358	498	459	199- 2	78	33	553	7.8
TOTALS	609	16549	2274	5205	.489	1368	1896	.743	950	1888	2838	3018	1630-11	994	205	5922	9.7

NBA HIGHS HIGHS

	14	25		13	16				17	17		6	4	39	

3-POINT FIELD GOALS: 1983-84, 4-15 (.267); 1984-85, 0-17 (.000); 1985-86, 0-10 (.000); 1986-87, 0-10 (.000); 1987-88, 0-6 (.000); 1988-89, 0-9 (.000), 1989-90, 2-21 (.095). 1990-91, 0-9 (.000).
CAREER: 6-91 (.065).

NBA PLAYOFF RECORD

TEAM-YR	GP	MIN	FGM	FGA	PCT.	FTM	FTA	PCT.	OFF	DEF	REB	AS	PF-DQ	ST	BL	PTS	AVE.
N.Y. '84	12	195	27	73	.370	28	46	.609	29	15	35	20	29- 0	24	2	82	6.8
DEN. '87	3	68	11	34	.324	4	7	.571	3	7	10	5	4- 0	2	0	26	8.7
WASH.'88	5	155	22	54	.407	11	16	.688	9	15	24	14	18- 0	7	4	55	11.0
TOTALS	20	418	60	161	.373	43	69	.623	41	37	69	39	51- 0	33	6	163	8.2

PLAYOFF HIGHS

	8	17		7	20				9	7				20	

3-POINT FIELD GOALS: 1987-88, 0-1 (.000).

ORLANDO WOOLRIDGE

Position: Forward
Height: 6'9"
Weight: 215
College: Notre Dame
High School: Mansfield (Mansfield, LA)
Birthdate: 12/16/59
Birthplace: Mansfield, LA
When Drafted: 1981 (1st round)
How Acquired: Trade
Pro Experience: 10 Years
Married: Patricia
Children: Zachary

LAST SEASON: Acquired from the Denver Nuggets in exchange for Scott Hastings and Detroit's 1992 second-round draft choice...The deal was part of a three-team trade which also included Jeff Martin coming to the Pistons and James Edwards going to the Clippers...Last season with the Nuggets, Woolridge averaged 25.1 points per game...However, he played in just 53 games, due to a detached retina injury...A 10-year NBA veteran, enjoyed his highest scoring average of his career...His 25.1 points per game would have ranked him 10th in the NBA in scoring last season, but he did not qualify because he played in only 53 games...Eclipsed the 10,000 career point total last season while a member of the Nuggets...

AS A PRO: Detroit is his fifth NBA stop while beginning his 11th campaign...Began his NBA career in Chicago playing his first five seasons with the Bulls...Since then has made stops in New Jersey, Los Angeles Lakers, Denver and now Detroit...Has averaged double figures in eight of his 10 NBA seasons...After playing five season in Chicago, he became a free agent and signed with New Jersey...In his second season with New Jersey (1987-88), he voluntarily entered a drug treatment center in Van Nuys, California in late February...He then missed the remainder of that season...Signed by the Lakers on August 10, 1988 where he played for two seasons, including a trip to the 1989 NBA Finals against the Pistons...Traded by the Lakers to Denver on August 3, 1990 in exchange for two second-round draft choices...

COLLEGE CAREER: Collegiate teammate at Notre Dame with Bill Laimbeer and former Piston Kelly Tripucka...Averaged 10.6 points for the Fighting Irish during his career...Notre Dame entered the NCAA Tournament in each of his four seasons posting a cumulative record of 92-26...Named second team All-American by The Sporting News as a senior, while earning honorable mention for U.P.I.

PERSONAL: Received his Degree from Notre Dame in Economics...Cousin of former Knicks' star and current Nets' V.P. Willis Reed...Self-professed health nut...

NBA CAREER RECORD

TEAM-YR	GP	MINS	FGM	FGA	PCT.	FTM	FTA	PCT.	OFF	DEF	REBS	AST	PF-DQ	STE	BLO	PTS.	AVE.
CHI.'82	75	1188	202	394	.513	144	206	.699	82	145	227	81	152- 1	23	24	548	7.3
CHI.'83	57	1627	361	622	.580	217	340	.638	122	176	298	97	177- 1	38	44	939	16.5
CHI.'84	75	2544	570	1086	.525	303	424	.715	130	239	369	136	253- 6	71	60	1444	19.3
CHI.'85	77	2816	679	1225	.554	409	521	.785	158	277	435	135	185- 0	58	38	1767	22.9
CHI.'86	70	2248	540	1090	.495	364	462	.788	150	200	350	213	186- 2	49	47	1448	20.7
NJ. '87	75	2638	556	1067	.521	438	564	.777	118	249	367	261	243- 4	54	86	1551	20.7
NJ. '88	19	622	110	247	.445	92	130	.708	31	60	91	71	73- 2	13	20	312	16.4
LA. '89	74	1491	231	494	.468	253	343	.738	81	189	270	58	130- 0	30	65	715	9.7
LA. '90	62	1421	306	550	.556	176	240	.733	49	136	185	96	160- 2	39	46	788	12.7
DEN.'91	53	1823	490	983	.498	350	439	.797	141	220	361	119	145- 2	69	23	1330	25.1
TOTALS	637	18418	4045	7758	.521	2746	3669	.748	1062	1891	2953	1267	1704-20	444	453	10842	17.0

NBA HIGHS

	18	28		15	20				16	10				44	

3-POINT FIELD GOALS: 1981-82, 0-3 (.000); 1982-83, 0-3 (.000); 1983-84, 1-2 (.500); 1984-85, 0-5 (.000); 1985-86, 4-23 (.174); 1986-87, 1-8 (.125); 1987-88, 0-2 (.000); 1988-89, 0-1 (.000), 1989-90, 0-5 (.000). 1990-91, 0-4 (.000).
CAREER: 6-56 (.107).

NBA PLAYOFF RECORD

TEAM-YR	GP	MIN	FGM	FGA	PCT.	FTM	FTA	PCT.	OFF	DEF	REB	AST	PF-DQ	ST	BL	PTS	AVE.
CHI. '85	4	167	34	68	.500	14	18	.778	6	7	13	8	19- 1	6	1	82	20.5
CHI. '86	3	135	25	62	.403	13	15	.867	6	8	14	4	12- 0	3	1	63	21.0
LA. '89	15	276	39	75	.520	44	62	.710	20	50	70	17	35- 0	2	15	122	8.1
LA. '90	9	199	40	70	.571	26	37	.703	6	17	23	10	25- 1	8	8	106	11.8
TOTALS	31	777	138	275	.502	97	132	.735	38	82	120	39	91- 2	19	25	373	12.0

PLAYOFF HIGHS

	11	27		8	8				9			28

3-POINT FIELD GOALS: 1985-86, 0-1 (.000).
CAREER 0-1 (.000).

LANCE BLANKS

Position: Guard
Height: 6'4"
Weight: 195
College: Texas '90
High School: McCullough HS, The Woodlands, TX
Birthdate: 09/09/66
Birthplace: Houston, TX
When Drafted: First Round (26th Overall), Detroit, 1990
Hou Acquired: College Draft
Pro Experience: One Year
Marital Status: Single
Residence: Houston, TX

LAST SEASON: Was not a member of the Pistons' playoff roster during his rookie campaign...Played in a total 37 games and averaged 1.7 points per game...Placed on the injured list March 3 with a groin pull, also limiting his number of appearances...

AS A COLLEGIAN: Selected by the Pistons (26th overall) in the first round of the 1990 NBA Draft...Averaged 20.3 points, 4.3 rebounds and 3.0 assists as a senior to help lead the Longhorns to the Midwest Regional Finals in the NCAA Tournament...Finished eighth on the all-time University of Texas scoring list with 1,322 points...His 20.0 scoring average was the third highest in school history...Sat out the 1987-88 season after transferring from Virginia where he saw limited action during his two seasons with the Cavaliers...

PERSONAL: His father Sid, a former NFL player, represents his son in contract negotiations...

NBA CAREER RECORD

TEAM-YR	GP	MINS	FGM	FGA	PCT.	FTM	FTA	PCT.	OFF	DEF	REBS	AVE.	AST	PF-DQ	STE	BLO	PTS.	AVE.
DET.'91	38	214	26	61	.426	10	14	.714	4	16	20	4.0	26	35- 0	9	2	64	1.7

3-POINT FIELD GOALS: 1990-91, 2-16 (.125).

JEFF MARTIN

Position: Guard
Height: 6'5"
Weight: 195
College: Murray State
When Drafted: 1989 (31st overall)
How Acquired: Trade
Pro Experience: Two Years

LAST SEASON: Acquired from the Los Angeles Clippers on August 13,1991 in a three-way deal which also included the Denver Nuggets...Came to the Pistons for James Edwards with the Pistons also receiving the Clippers' 1995 second-round draft choice...Orlando Woolridge was acquired from Denver in the same deal which also sent Scott Hastings to the Nuggets...Averaged 7.1 points per game with the Clippers last season, his second campaign in the NBA...Started 26 games last season...Scored his career high 25 points at Utah on Dec. 29, 1990...

AS A PRO: Was the 31st pick of the Clippers in the 1989 NBA draft...Has started 49 games through his first two NBA seasons...Was a starting guard for the Clippers through the final two months of his rookie season...Has averaged 6.7 points per game through his first two NBA campaigns...

AS A COLLEGIAN: Named Ohio Valley Conference Player of the Year in 1989 after averaging 25.6 points per game for Murray State...Owns 12 Murray State records including career scoring leader...Three-time Ohio Valley First Team selection...Twice was named the Ohio Valley Male Athlete of the Year...Started 116 of 117 games played at Murray State...

PERSONAL: Like Joe Dumars, he also comes from a family with a football background...Older brother Wayne was a 1989 first-round draft choice of the New Orleans Saints...The street his family lives on in Cherry Valley, Arkansas was renamed Martin Drive for the two brothers' accomplishments...Was the first Ohio Valley Conference player to attend the 1988 Olympic Trials...Majored in Safety Engineering at Murray State...

NBA CAREER RECORD

TEAM-YR	GP	MINS	FGM	FGA	PCT.	FTM	FTA	PCT.	OFF	DEF	REBS	AST	PF-DQ	STE	BLO	PTS.	AVE.
LAC. '90	69	1351	170	414	.411	91	129	.705	78	81	159	44	97- 0	41	16	433	6.3
LAC.'91	74	1334	214	507	.422	68	100	.680	53	78	131	65	104- 0	37	31	523	7.1
TOTALS	143	2685	384	921	.417	159	229	.694	131	159	290	109	201- 0	78	47	956	6.7

NBA HIGHS

	49		9	18		8	10					12	5			25	

3-POINT FIELD GOALS: 1989-90, 2-15 (.133); 1990-91, 27-88 (.307). CAREER: 29-103 (.282).

DOUG OVERTON

Position: Guard
Height: 6'3"
Weight: 190
College: LaSalle
When Drafted: 1991 (2nd, 40)
How Acquired: Draft
Pro Experience: Rookie

LAST SEASON: Averaged 22.3 points, 4.1 rebounds, 5.0 assists during his senior season at LaSalle...Scored his career-high 45 points against Loyola Marymount, combining with teammate Randy Woods for an NCAA-record 91 points in that game...Named the Most Valuable Player of Daiwa (Tokyo) tournament...

AS A COLLEGIAN: LaSalle's all-time leader in assists (671) and steals (277), second in games played (123) and sixth among all-time scorers (1,795)...Selected to All-MAAC team for three straight seasons...In his four seasons at LaSalle, the team recorded a 99-28 record...

COLLEGE CAREER RECORD

YEAR	GP	FGM	FGA	PCT.	FTM	FTA	PCT.	REB	AST	PTS	AVE.
LASALLE '88	34	110	221	.498	37	44	.841	81	91	265	7.8
LASALLE '89	32	174	352	.494	47	59	.787	101	244	421	13.2
LASALLE '90	32	201	387	.519	95	119	.798	133	212	551	17.2
LASALLE '91	25	199	447	.445	106	128	.818	103	124	558	22.3
TOTALS	123	684	1407	.486	285	350	.814	418	671	1795	14.6

BRAD SELLERS

Position: Forward
Height: 7'8"
Weight: 218
When Drafted: 1986
How Acquired: Free Agent
Pro Experience: Five Years

LAST SEASON: Spent the 1990-91 campaign playing in Greece for a team in the city of Thessaloniki...Was signed as an unrestricted free agent by the Pistons on August 21, 1991...

AS A PRO: Detroit becomes his fourth NBA stop...Began his NBA career in Chicago, playing three seasons with the Bulls from 1986 through 1989...Traded by Chicago to Seattle for a 1989 first-round draft choice on June 26, 1989...During the middle of the 1989-90 campaign, he was traded by Seattle to Minnesota for Steve Johnson and a 1991 second-round draft choice...Had three productive seasons with Chicago, averaging 8.3 points per game during his stint as a Bull...Scored 27 points in his first NBA start, ironically versus the Pistons...He was selected one pick prior to Detroit's John Salley in the 1986 Draft...

AS A COLLEGIAN: Only the seventh player in Big Ten history to top 1,000 points and 1,000 rebounds...Played his first season at Wisconsin before transfering to Ohio State...Most Valuable Player in the 1986 National Invitational Tournament...

PERSONAL: Returned to Ohio State after his collegiate playing days to gain his degree in Economics...Makes his year-round home in Cleveland...

NBA CAREER RECORD

TEAM-YR	GP	MINS	FGM	FGA	PCT.	FTM	FTA	PCT.	OFF	DEF	REBS	AST	PF-DQ	STE	BLO	PTS	AVE.
CHI.'87	80	1751	276	606	.455	126	173	.728	155	218	373	102	194- 1	44	68	680	8.5
CHI.'88	82	2212	326	714	.457	124	157	.790	107	143	250	141	174- 0	34	66	777	9.5
CHI.'89	80	1732	231	476	.485	86	101	.851	85	142	227	99	176- 2	35	69	551	6.9
SEA.MIN.90	59	700	103	254	.406	58	73	.795	39	50	89	33	74- 1	17	22	264	4.5
TOTALS	301	6395	936	2050	.457	394	504	.782	386	553	939	375	618- 4	130	225	2272	7.5

NBA HIGHS

14	25		9	12				13	8				32

3-POINT FIELD GOALS: 1986-87, 2-10 (.200); 1987-88, 1-7 (.143); 1988-89, 3-6 (.500); 1989-90, 0-5 (.000). CAREER: 6-28 (.214).

NBA PLAYOFF RECORD

TEAM-YR	GP	MIN	FGM	FGA	PCT.	FTM	FTA	PCT.	OFF	DEF	REB	AST	PF-DQ	ST	BL	PTS	AVE.
CHI.'87	3	68	6	19	.316	3	3	1.000	2	5	7	3	8- 0	0	1	15	5.0
CHI.'88	10	144	15	43	.349	15	17	.882	10	11	21	8	18- 0	2	5	45	4.5
CHI.'89	13	177	22	58	.379	10	12	.883	15	16	31	15	21- 0	3	4	54	4.2
TOTALS	26	389	43	120	.358	28	32	.875	27	32	59	26	47- 0	5	10	114	4.4

PLAYOFF HIGHS

8	8					7	3	22

** NOTE 1990-91 SEASON PLAYED IN GREECE

PISTONS ALL-TIME RECORDS AGAINST NBA OPPONENTS 1957-1991

TEAM	79-80	80-81	81-82	82-83	83-84	84-85	85-86	86-87	87-88	88-89	89-90	90-91	TOTAL	HOME	ROAD	NEUTRAL
ATL*	0-6	2-4	4-2	3-3	4-2	5-1	2-4	3-3	4-2	5-1	2-3	5-0	109-133	58-51	40-68	11-14
BOS	0-6	1-4	0-6	3-3	3-3	2-4	1-4	2-3	3-3	3-1	2-2	2-2	55-157	33-66	17-66	5-25
CHA	—	—	—	—	—	—	—	—	—	4-0	2-0	4-1	10-1	5-0	5-1	—
CHI	1-1	1-5	6-0	4-2	5-1	3-3	4-2	3-3	4-2	6-0	4-1	2-3	83-65	52-20	29-43	2-2
CLE	0-6	3-3	5-1	5-1	5-1	5-1	5-1	5-1	5-1	3-3	4-1	3-2	69-36	39-16	30-20	—
DAL	—	2-0	1-1	0-2	2-0	2-0	2-0	1-1	1-1	2-0	1-1	2-0	16-6	9-2	7-4	—
DEN	1-1	0-2	1-1	0-2	1-1	2-0	1-1	2-0	1-1	1-1	2-0	2-0	19-17	11-7	8-10	—
GS#	1-1	0-2	2-0	2-0	1-1	2-0	1-1	1-1	2-0	1-1	1-1	1-1	79-105	49-32	23-53	7-20
HOU	1-5	1-1	2-0	2-0	1-1	1-1	1-1	1-1	1-1	1-1	1-1	2-0	48-39	31-10	13-28	4-1
IND	1-5	2-4	2-4	4-2	4-2	6-0	5-1	3-3	3-3	4-2	4-1	3-2	46-36	31-10	15-26	—
LAC!	0-2	1-1	2-0	1-1	2-0	1-1	2-0	2-0	1-1	2-0	1-1	2-0	43-21	25-7	18-14	—
LAL%	0-2	0-2	0-2	0-2	1-1	1-1	1-1	1-1	0-2	2-0	1-1	0-2	73-128	32-54	26-62	15-12
MIA	—	—	—	—	—	—	—	—	—	2-0	3-1	3-1	8-2	5-0	3-2	—
MIL	1-1	1-5	2-4	3-3	3-2	3-3	2-4	3-3	4-2	2-4	3-2	2-3	52-79	35-30	17-47	0-2
MIN	—	—	—	—	—	—	—	—	—	—	2-0	2-0	4-0	2-0	2-0	—
NJ	2-4	3-3	2-4	3-2	1-4	1-5	4-2	5-1	5-1	4-0	4-0	3-1	43-33	24-14	19-19	—
NY	2-4	1-5	3-3	1-5	4-2	3-2	4-1	6-0	4-2	0-4	4-0	1-3	97-118	53-45	32-61	12-12
ORL	—	—	—	—	—	—	—	—	—	—	5-0	2-0	7-0	4-0	3-0	—
PHIL+	1-5	1-4	2-3	0-6	3-3	1-5	2-4	5-0	4-1	5-0	1-3	2-2	79-135	48-45	18-70	13-20
PHOE	0-2	0-2	0-2	1-1	2-0	2-0	0-2	1-1	2-0	2-0	2-0	0-2	40-41	24-17	15-24	1-0
PORT	0-2	0-2	0-2	1-1	1-1	1-1	1-1	1-1	0-2	1-1	1-1	1-1	33-32	23-10	10-22	—
SAC$	0-2	1-1	2-0	0-2	1-1	1-1	1-1	0-2	1-1	2-0	2-0	2-0	106-96	62-21	28-51	16-24
SA	2-4	0-2	0-2	1-1	1-1	1-1	1-1	1-1	1-1	2-0	1-1	0-2	14-24	7-12	7-12	—
SEA	0-2	0-2	1-1	0-2	1-1	1-1	2-0	2-0	1-1	2-0	1-1	1-1	42-41	26-14	11-27	5-0
UTAH@	1-1	0-2	1-1	0-2	1-1	0-2	1-1	1-1	2-0	2-0	1-1	0-2	23-21	15-7	8-14	—
WASH=	2-4	1-5	2-0	3-2	3-3	3-3	4-2	3-3	3-2	5-0	4-0	3-1	90-93	50-29	26-55	14-9
TOTALS	16-66	21-61	39-43	37-45	49-33	46-36	46-36	52-30	54-28	63-19	59-23	50-32	1288-1459	753-519	430-799	105-141

*ST. lOUIS 1957-68   #PHILADELPHIA 1957-62, SAN FRANCISCO 1962-79 $CINCINNATI 1957-72   KANSAS CITY 1972-85   %MINNEAPOLIS 1957-60   +SYRACUSE 1957-63   !BUFFALO 1970-78
SANDIEGO 1979-84, @NEW ORLEANS 1974-79   =CHICAGO 1961-63, BALTIMORE 1963-74   #PHILADELPHIA 1957-62, SAN FRANCISCO 1962-79.

WILLIAM DAVIDSON

MANAGING PARTNER

Recognized as one of the most successful owners in the NBA, Pistons Managing Partner William Davidson can be credited for a majority of the success the organization now enjoys. Detroit's 1989 and 1990 World Championships can be directly attributed to Davidson, the club's majority owner since 1974 and under Davidson's direction, the Pistons have been considered one of league's elite franchises for the last five years.

The future of the organization has never looked brighter. With the recent purchase of The New Pine Knob, Arena Associates (Davidson's company) now has the ability to bring summer entertainment to its clientele. In 1988-89, the Pistons began play in The Palace of Auburn Hills, a state-of-the-art arena built with Davidson's financial support. Also under Davidson's supervision, is the construction of a new outdoor theatre, The Palace Gardens, which will bring the very best in summer concerts to the area.

The Pistons are coming off the five most successful seasons in the history of the franchise.For the first time in the last four years, the Pistons did not advance to the NBA Finals and did not finish first in the central division. The team did, however, win 50 games during the regular season. The Pistons are the only team, along with the Los Angeles Lakers, to win 50+ games over the las three seasons.

Davidson acquired the Detroit Pistons in 1974 from the late Fred Zollner, the man who founded the team in Fort Wayne in the 1940's and moved the franchise to Detroit before the 1957-58season.

Interested in a wide variety of sports, Davidson is one of the most knowledgeable heads of an NBA franchise. He can usually be found sitting courtside at all Pistons home games, and has studied the talents and abilities of players and coaches in the league and is able to make some very astute observations.

The Pistons' majority owner likes success and has known it in his business interests. That's why now, the success of the Detroit Pistons comes as no surprise to those who are aware of Davidson's ability to manage people. His secret is simple: Hire competent managers and place the responsibility with them.

Educated in Business Law, Davidson received a Bachelor's Degree in Business Administration from the University of Michigan and earned a Juris Doctor's Degree from Wayne State University.

After three years, Davidson gave up his law practice to take over a wholesale drug company. He rescued it from bankruptcy and turned it around in three years. After this success, he did the same with a surgical supply company. The next step was to take over the Guardian Glass Company, the family business, pay off all debts and head

it into the profitable direction the company now enjoys. Today, Guardian Industries remains the flagship of his business interests.

Davidson expects his previous track record to help pave the way for the Pistons, The Palace and The New Pine Knob. He hopes his formula for success, which turned the Pistons around and made The Palace one of the top arenas in the world, will carry over into The New Pine Knob undertaking.

Davidson's management talents are continually on display in NBA circles, where he is active on the player relations and finance committees. He was a member of the committee which selected former NBA Commissioner Lawrence O'Brien in 1975. Davidson is also active in many community and charitable affairs.

The athletic interests of William Davidson date back many years and have continued alongside his business career. He was a high school and college trackman and played freshman football in the Navy during World War II. Davidson was an inaugural inductee into the Jewish Sports Hall of Fame.

The Detroit Pistons ownership group includes Legal Counsel Oscar Feldman, and Advisory Board Members Warren Colville, Ted Ewald, Milt Dresner, Bud Gerson, Dorothy Gerson, David Mondry Eugene Mondry, Ann Newman, Herb Tyner and William Wetsman.

JACK McCLOSKEY

GENERAL MANAGER

Building from the ground up and making something out of nothing is one of the most difficult things in life to do. But for the past 13 season, that is exactly what Detroit Pistons General Manager, Jack McCloskey, has been doing. His keen basketball knowledge has built the Pistons into one of the elite franchises in the NBA with a solid "new" tradition.

Known throughout the NBA as "Trader Jack", McCloskey has the unique ability to make a trade and then have the involved player make an immediate contribution to the team. In 1988-89, his acquisition of Mark Aguirre added to his reputation, as the Pistons finished with a 45-8 record and won their first World Championship. Also, take into consideration his signing of three seasoned veterans for the Pistons 1989-90 Championship bench, and one can see why McCloskey is known as one of the best in the league.

When the Pistons needed an astute basketball mind to direct the on-court fortunes of the club, Managing Partner William Davidson appointed NBA veteran McCloskey as General Manager on December 11, 1979. Over those past eleven years, McCloskey's sometimes risky but effective trades have often been the talk of the league.

At the time of his arrival, Davidson called McCloskey's addition, "a positive step in the building of our franchise to an NBA Championship level." Since that statement, the Pistons have won two World Championships, three Eastern Conference titles and three Central Division crowns all a direct result of McCloskey's tirelessness and endless hours of hard work.

In each of the last five seasons, McCloskey has been mentioned among the top Executives of the Year in the league. With his ability to select top-notch collegiate talent through the NBA draft in addition to trades, McCloskey has been able to keep the Pistons ahead in the race to the NBA Title. McCloskey's duties include authority over all basketball-playing aspects of the Pistons organization including coaching, player personnel, all scouting and trades.

A native of Mahoney City, PA, McCloskey came to the Pistons from the Indiana Pacers where he was serving as an assistant to Head Coach Bob Leonard during the 1979-80 season. Previously, he assisted Jerry West, now General Manager of the Los Angeles Lakers, for three seasons. In his tenure with the Lakers, he served as the offensive coordinator for two seasons and defensive coordinator for a season, and the Lakers bounced back from two losing seasons with three winning campaigns.

Upon joining the Pistons, McCloskey, a 1948 graduate of the University of Pennsylvania, had 23 years of playing and coaching experience behind him. During his playing days, he was an acknowledged all-around athlete, participating in basketball and football at Penn. He then played eight years in the American and Eastern Basketball League. His career also included a brief stint in the NBA and four years of professional baseball in the Philadelphia A's organization. McCloskey and diminutive guard, Charlie Criss, are in the history books as the Eastern League's only two-time MVP's.

McCloskey began his coaching career in 1956, by returning to Penn and inheriting a 7-19 team. He turned the team around, going 13-12 and 12-14 and then recording seven straight winning seasons with Ivy League first division finishes annually. In his final season, McCloskey led the 1965-66 Penn team to a 19-6 campaign, the most wins since 1954-55, and captured the Ivy League Title. His teams were 87-53 in Ivy League play and won the Philadelphia Big Five Title in 1963, on their way to a 146-105 overall record in ten seasons.

McCloskey's next step was to transform a lowly Wake Forest team into an Atlantic Coast Conference contender. After a 14-39 mark in his first two seasons as the Deacons head coach, he followed with four successful seasons in the rugged ACC. With assistants Billy Packer and the late Neil Johnston, scoring ace for the old Warriors, McCloskey compiled a 56-50 record before moving to the NBA.

His next chore was the take over the expansion Portland Trailblazers in 1972-73 for two building seasons. The Pacific Division team was an eventual NBA Champion and ironically was the Pistons opponent during the 1989-90 Championship Series.

Jack and wife Leslie make their home in West Bloomfield. Jack was a 1981 inductee into the Jerry Wolman Chapter of the Pennsylvania Sports Hall of Fame. One of the top senior tennis players in the state, Jack was won several tournaments. In 1991, he was a gold medalist in the Senior Olympics for 3-on-3 basketball. Also in '91, McCloskey was inducted into the Philadelphia Sports Hall of Fame.

THOMAS S. WILSON

CHIEF EXECUTIVE OFFICER

Over the last eight seasons, the Detroit Pistons have been one of the most successfully marketed franchises in the National Basketball Association. That has been proven by the current all-time high interest mark in the club, setting league attendance records and high television and merchandising sales marks for the Pistons and the NBA. One of the major factors behind the financial success the Detroit Pistons now enjoy, is Chief Executive Officer, Thomas S. Wilson.

For the third straight year, the organization sold out every home game during the regular season and playoffs. The Pistons, as they begin the 1991-92 season, have now sold out 151 straight games.

Over the last 12 years with the Pistons, Wilson's duties and responsibilities have continued to increase dramatically. As the Pistons' Chief Executive Officer, Wilson oversees all the administrative, marketing, broadcasting and promotional efforts of the organization.

Wilson's workload increased dramatically with the opening of The Palace of Auburn Hills in 1988. The home of the two time World Champions, the arena was designed largely around Wilson's input. Wilson tried to combine the best aspects from individual arenas, throughout the United States and Canada. He had been studying arenas for three years prior to construction of The Palace. The Pistons were able to customize the facility, providing the finest sightlines and comfort levels for basketball of any arena in the country. Wilson was responsible for staffing the arena and developing the philosophies that present The Palace's events in the finest manner possible. He has developed a family-like atmosphere among the staff, giving patrons a feeling of being guests in someone's home, rather than spectators in an arena.

"The success of the Detroit Pistons has been very rewarding to the organization and to me personally, but the challenge of designing the finest facility ever built for basketball and other events has been the most exciting project I have ever been involved with," says Wilson.

To complicate matters further, in 1991 Wilson was named president of The New Pine Knob. His duties with the Pine Knob project mirror those of the Pistons and The Palace: overseeing all administrative, marketing, broadcasting and promotional efforts of the facility.

The Pistons, under Wilson's leadership, have led the league in attendance in four of the last seven years and set a league record of 61,983 fans for one game in 1988. The Pistons also set an all-time NBA record for attendance in 1987-88 becoming the first NBA franchise to attract one million fans during the regular season.

The Pistons' outstanding success in broadcasting is also headed by Wilson. When the Pistons moved both

the television and radio broadcast in-house, he was responsible for overseeing all aspects. Over the last four seasons, the Pistons have set franchise records in television ratings.

Wilson continues to be involved with broadcasting as he serves as color commentator for all Pistons' games on Pro-Am Sports Systems (PASS). For the last six seasons, and again in 1990-91, Wilson has teamed-up with Channel 4's Fred McLeod in telecasting the games on cable.

A native Detroiter, Wilson received his Bachelor's of Business Administration degree from Wayne State University. Prior to joining the Pistons, he worked for the Los Angeles Lakers and the Los Angeles Kings at the Great Western Forum. He also worked in films and television in California, appearing in over 40 television programs.

An avid golfer, Wilson spends most of the summer working on his game. He also likes to play tennis and has participated in two Free Press Marathons. Tom and his wife, Linda, reside in Rochester Hills with daughters Kasey and Brooke and new son Kevin.

CHUCK DALY

HEAD COACH

Chuck Daly has taken his place in Detroit Pistons franchise history as well as NBA history. For the NBA, Daly is only the third coach in history to record back-to-back world championships. For the Pistons, Daly is the most successful coach in the team's 32 years of existence.

Before he came to Detroit in 1983, the Pistons had never recorded back-to-back winning seasons. All that has changed in Daly's eight years, as the Pistons have not had a losing season since and have made the playoffs in each season of his tenure.

In 1991, Daly guided the Pistons to a third straight 50 win season and a berth in the Eastern Conference Finals. Daly, with a 69-39 record, is second on the list of winningest active coaches in the playoffs behind New York's Pat Riley.

In 1990, the Pistons set the top two winning streaks in franchise history. During the months of January, February and March the Pistons won 13 games and then 12 in a row with only one loss in between. The 25-1 streak was the third best in the history of the NBA and lasted from January 23 through March 21.

The Pistons have now enjoyed the five best seasons in the clubs history under Daly's direction (1987, '88,'89,'90 and '91). During Daly's term as head coach, the Pistons have won three Eastern Conference titles, three central division titles and two World Championships. Prior to his arrival, the Pistons had never won a central division title. His eight year regular season record with Detroit now stands at 419-247.

On February 15, 1991, the USA Basketball committee announced that Daly would be the coach of the 1992 USA Olympic men's basketball team.

"I've had a lot of good things happen to me in basketball," Daly said. "We won two NBA Titles and I went to the Final Four as an assistant. But this honor (Olympics) is right up there. It's something you don't dream will ever happen to you."

The 1992 Olympics mark the first time that professional players will be allowed to compete.

"It's the ultimate challenge in that you're assembling a team of the greatest basketball talent ever," Daly said of how a decision will be made on the team. "I expect to come back from Barcelona with the gold medal."

Daly was named the head coach of the Pistons on May 17, 1983 replacing Scotty Robertson. In his first season with the club in 1983-84, Daly improved their record by 12 games, as the Pistons finished with a 49-33 mark and a post season appearance. Then in the next two campaigns, the team finished with 46-36 records and post-season appearances. The Pistons went on to enjoy the most successful seasons in the history of the franchise in Daly's fourth, fifth, sixth, seventh and eighth seasons.

His more than 30 years of success at all levels of coaching easily carried over into his Pistons position. Prior to joining the Pistons, Daly spent four-plus season as an assistant to Billy Cunningham and the Philadelphia 76ers. The Sixers were 236-104 in regular-season play during those four-plus years, winning two division titles

and finishing second twice. The Sixers also logged a 32-21 playoff record in the four seasons before he departed for the Cleveland Cavaliers' head coaching job. Daly was regarded by the Sixers as especially adept at setting up offenses and defenses for particular opponents.

In Daly's six seasons (1971-77) as the head coach of the University of Pennsylvania, his teams won four Ivy League titles and were runners-up twice. Penn won three Big Fiver Championships outright and tied for another under Daly's supervision, while compiling an overall record of 125-38 (.744 percentage) and won 20 of 25 Big Five Titles (.800 percentage). In his first season as the Penn head coach, he led the Quakers to a 25-3 record, a No. 3 ranking nationally and first place in the Eastern Collegiate Athletic Conference (ECAC). Daly led Penn to more NCAA berths and Big Five titles than any other head coach at Penn.

Daly was the head coach at Boston College for two seasons (1969-71) with a 26-26 record. He had served as an assistant at Duke for seven years (1963-69), first as freshman coach and then four years as the varsity assistant coach.

A graduate of Bloomsburg University, after starting his collegiate career at St. Bonaventure, Daly earned a Master's Degree at Penn State and began his coaching career at Punxsutawney High School.

Daly, a native of Kane, Pennsylvania, has become a very popular speaker on the banquet circuit and has numerous endorsements with sponsors. He is the co-host of the very popular television show "The Chuck and Bernie Show" with local sports personality Bernie Smilovitz. He loves to spend his time on the golf course during the summer and also enjoys mystery novels.

Chuck, and his wife Terry, reside in West Bloomfield. they have one daughter, Cydney, a Penn State graduate who works for Revlon.

WILL ROBINSON

ADMINISTRATIVE ASSISTANT TO THE GENERAL MANAGER

Will Robinson has dedicated his life to the sport of basketball. Recently, the game has been returning the favor as the Robinson legacy continues.

Receiving his second Championship ring in 1990, Robinson has truly reached the pinnacle of the sport that has been his life for over 50 years. Currently, Robinson is the right hand man to General Manager, Jack McCloskey with duties that include scouting, special assignments for the basketball staff and director of the Pistons' Training Camp.

It was through his efforts, along with scout Stan Novak, that the Detroit Pistons built a team that would become only the third in history to repeat as World Champions. He had enough insight to see talent in the likes of Dennis Rodman, Joe Dumars and John Salley and convinced McCloskey to make them Pistons.

In the spring of 1982, Robinson was inducted into the Michigan Sports Hall of Fame, marking the supreme honor in the state where he enjoyed the majority of his coaching success. The list of athletes that have played for Robinson reads like a Who's Who in sports. His teams were usually tagged with the title "Champion."

Robinson enjoyed success at Detroit Miller High School where his 1947 team won the city championship over St. Joseph's High School. The game drew 16,249 to Olympia Stadium, a State of Michigan attendance mark until the Pistons moved to the Pontiac Silverdome in 1978.

Moving to Pershing High School, Robinson brought successful basketball with him, as his teams racked up several championships and won at an 85 percent clip.

One of the strongest high school teams ever assembled played for Robinson in the 1967 season. The five all later played in professional sports. Spencer Haywood and Ralph Simpson (both NBA and ABA), Glen Doughty and Paul Seals (pro football) and Marvin Lane (major league baseball) won the State Championship that year.

Great talent usually does not go unnoticed and in Robinson's case the talent was recognized. Illinois State Athletic Director, Milt Weisbecker, gave Robinson his shot at the big-time and made him the first black coach in major college history. ISU teams recorded five consecutive winning seasons and produced such standouts as All-Pro guard Doug Collins and Bubbles Hawkins, who was an Olympian as well as a successful NBA guard.

There have been other standouts like Wayne State all-time great Charlie Primas, Baltimore Colt All-Pro Big Daddy Lipscomb, Wayne State VP Noah Brown, and Olympians Lorenzo Wright, Charley Fonville. The athletic field was not the only place where Robinson's influence was shown. He is just as proud of the good people he

produced such as Ofield Dukes, a political advisor, the 25 Detroit police officers who played for him and the college grads with PhD's attached to their names. Many of the sons of players that Robinson coached are now making headlines themselves.

Robinson's induction into the Michigan Sports Hall of Fame marked the seventh such honor bestowed him. The other include: the Michigan High School Coaches Hall of Fame, The West Virginia State Hall of Fame, The Illinois State Hall of Fame, The Upper Ohio Valley Dapper Dan Hall of Fame, The Afro American Sports Hall of Fame and the Michigan High School Basketball Hall of Fame.

Robinson, who makes his home in Detroit, has one son, William Jr., the Coordinator of Equal Opportunity Programs at the University of Michigan.

STAN NOVAK

DIRECTOR OF SCOUTING

With over 40 years of pro basketball experience behind him, Stan Novak enters his 12th season as the Pistons' Director of Scouting.

Novak's knowledge of basketball, along with his keen ability to assess talent, has helped the Pistons to develop one of the strongest teams in the history of the league. It was his input that brought key contributors such as Joe Dumars, John Salley and Dennis Rodman to the Detroit Pistons.

Though an integral cog in the Piston's system, he is not often in the Detroit area. His life is spent on the road, traveling around the country and, most recently, the world scouting games and evaluating pro prospects. He is also actively involved in assisting with the Piston's Rookie/Free Agent camp and pre-season training camp.

Novak has seen the Pistons undergo a metamorphosis since joining the organization in the 1979-80 season. The Pistons lost 66 games that year and were lacking in all areas. Since that time, Novak has had a hand in forming the Pistons nucleus of Isiah Thomas, Bill Laimbeer and

Dumars and has been given the task of finding strong players that will fit into the Pistons team concept.

Prior to joining the Pistons, Novak's background included 31 years as a professional coach in the CBA. He began as a player/coach for Sunbury in 1949. His teammates included Pistons GM Jack McCloskey and legendary coach Jack Ramsey. Novak also coached in Trenton, Wilkes-Barne, Scranton, Allentown and Lancaster. Before his CBA career, Novak coached for 18 years at the high school level at Springfield Township High School. His teams won a cumulative 85% of their games.

Philadelphia born and educated, Novak graduated from West Philadelphia High School and the University of Pennsylvania. He is part of the Penn pipeline to Detroit which includes Head Coach Chuck Daly, McCloskey and himself. Stan was the captain of the Penn basketball team and enjoys tennis with long time friend Jack McCloskey.

BRENDAN SUHR

ASSISTANT COACH

Beginning his third season as top assistant for Chuck Daly and the Detroit Pistons is 12-year NBA veteran, Brendan Suhr.

Suhr joined the Pistons in January of the 1988-89 season when then top assistant, Dick Versace, left to take over the head coaching duties for the Indiana Pacers. With the Pistons, Suhr had won two Eastern Conference titles and two World Championships.

Suhr is considered one of the top technicians in the game and specializes in designing offenses and defenses that will neutralize Pistons opponents. He is one of the best teachers in the league and will be on the bench for every game with duties that include practice and game coaching as well as advance scouting. He also runs the Pistons rookie/free agent camps during the summer and has a big role in developing young talent.

Before joining Chuck Daly's staff, Suhr served as Assistant General Manager and Director of Scouting for the Atlanta Hawks. He joined the Hawks in the 1979-80 season as an assistant coach and held that position for nine consecutive NBA seasons before being appointed Asst. General Manager in July of 1988.

In college, Suhr was a standout guard and led his Montclair State team to two NCAA Tournament berths. As a senior, he was named team captain and most valuable player. Also as a senior, he led his team in assists and was second in the nation in free throw percentage.

After graduation, Brendan spent one season as an assistant at the University of Detroit before moving to Fairfield University (CT). At Fairfield he earned his Masters Degree in Educational Administration in 1979. Six years of college coaching saw his teams compile a 106-57 cumulative record and a berth in the 1978 NIT Tournament for Fairfield.

Suhr and his wife, Brenda, have two children, Christina and Brendan Kelly (B.K.) and make their home in the Rochester area. Brendan is one of the NBA's most dedicated distance runners and spends much of his time in the off season with basketball camps and clinics.

BRENDAN MALONE

ASSISTANT COACH

Brendan Malone, a 20-year coaching veteran, begins his 4th season as an assistant to Chuck Daly, completing one of the most successful triumvirates in the NBA.

Malone, one of the most well-liked men in the NBA, replaced Ron Rothstein in 1988 when Rothstein took over head coaching responsibilities for the Miami Heat. Malone's duties for the Pistons include advance scouting of all opponents, game and practice responsibilities and player development.

He is considered an excellent basketball man and very knowledgeable concerning the technical aspects of the NBA. Malone is an outstanding teacher and is entrusted with job of advising players on shooting, rebounding and developing their skills.

Before joining the Pistons, Malone was an assistant coach and scout for the New York Knicks under Hubie Brown. His duties with the Knicks were similar to his current duties. With the Knicks Malone learned discipline and how to be one of the most prepared men in the NBA.

Malone joined the Knickerbockers in 1986, following a two-year stint as the head coach at the University of Rhode Island, beginning in 1984.

Prior to coaching at Rhode Island, Malone was an assistant coach under Jim Boeheim at Syracuse University for six seasons. From 1978 through 1984, the Orangemen posted a record of 134-52 (72 percent) and made three NCAA Tournament appearances.

He began his coaching career at Power Memorial Academy in New York City where he remained for 10 successful seasons. In Malone's final six seasons at Power Memorial, his teams won a pair of City Championships, and he was a three-time new York City "Coach of the Year."

Malone played high school basketball at Rice High School in New York City and then in college at Iona University. Malone went on to earn his Master's Degree in Physical Education at New York University. He and his wife, Maureen, reside in Birmingham and have six children.

MIKE ABDENOUR

ATHLETIC TRAINER

Mike Abdenour, a Detroit native, begins his 15th season as Head Trainer for the Pistons. Certified by the National Athletic Trainers' Association, the 39-year old Abdenour holds a Bachelor's Degree from Wayne State and is in the process of completing his Master's Degree.

As a trainer, Abdenour is well-versed on the rigors of basketball and what it takes to stay in top condition. He served as student trainer for four years at Detroit Denby High School and then two years, while still a student, at Macomb County Community College. After a three-year apprenticeship at Wayne State under long time Pistons consultant, Bob White, Abdenour broke in with the team as Bud Shockro's assistant.

Mike's responsibilities go far beyond the usual taping of ankles and mending of bruises one associates with a

trainer. His job is a year-round occupation. He oversees all off-season conditioning programs for players and is an integral part of rookie/free agent camp during the summer, as well as training camp in October. He is responsible for preparing all team travel arrangements during the season including hotel accommodations and ground transportation when the Pistons are on the road.

Mike's brother, Tom, is also a trainer in the NBA working for the Golden State Warriors. Mike was chosen to accompany a Players' Association trip to China and served as Head Trainer for the Eastern Conference in the 1979 All-Star game at the Silverdome. Mike received a third ring this summer as he was married in August. Mike and his new bride, the former Janice Johnston, reside in

Mike works on Joe.